THE REAL READER'S QUARTERLY

Slightly Foxed

'Dreaming of the Bosphorus'

NO.37   SPRING 2013

Editors Gail Pirkis and Hazel Wood
Marketing and publicity Stephanie Allen and Jennie Paterson
Subscriptions Alarys Gibson, Anna Kirk and Faith McAllister

Cover illustration: Carry Akroyd, 'Fox and Rapefields', watercolour

Carry Akroyd is a painter and printmaker. She lives in Northamptonshire and so, being as far away as possible from all National Parks and Areas of Outstanding Natural Beauty, has chosen landscape as her subject matter. She has written a book about her work, *'Nature's Powers & Spells': Landscape Change, John Clare and Me*. For more about her work see www.carryakroyd.co.uk.

Design by Octavius Murray

Layout by Andrew Evans

Colophon and tailpiece by David Eccles

Published by Slightly Foxed Limited
53 Hoxton Square
London N1 6PB

tel 020 7033 0258
fax 0870 1991245
e-mail all@foxedquarterly.com
www.foxedquarterly.com

Slightly Foxed is published quarterly in early March, June, September and December
Annual subscription rates (4 issues)
UK £40; Europe £48; Rest of the World £52
Single copies of this issue can be bought for £10 (UK), £12 (Europe) or £13 (Rest of the World)
Back issues are also available

ISBN 978-1-906562-46-5
Printed and bound by Smith Settle, Yeadon, West Yorkshire

Contents

From the Editors   5

Dreaming of the Bosphorus · ATES ORGA   7

Common Sense Dancing · ALLISON PEARSON   12

The Sound of Youth · WILLIAM PALMER   18

A World of Words · ANNABEL WALKER   23

Pillow Talk · OLIVER PRITCHETT   28

Map Magic · C. J. SCHÜLER   32

The Wild Ginger Man · ANDREW NIXON   39

With a Notebook and a Ukulele · GORDON BOWKER   45

Putting the Hum into the Humdrum · A. F. HARROLD   50

Adventures in Achromatopsia · CATHERINE MERRICK   56

Flashman's Nemesis · BRIAN PAYNE   61

Hurricane Clarice · MICHAEL MARETT-CROSBY   64

Contents

The Man in the Lavender Suit · DEREK PARKER 69

Of Bembo, Caslon and Clairvaux · ROGER HUDSON 75

Talking to the Major · DENNIS BUTTS 81

Wells of Memory · CHRISTIAN TYLER 86

Shop with a Heart · MARIE FORSYTH 91

Bibliography 95

Ann Tout, 'Hedgehog'

Our bookshop can obtain any of the books mentioned in this issue.
Slightly Foxed on Gloucester Road, 123 Gloucester Road,
London sw7 4TE, e-mail: enquiries@foxedbooks.com, tel: 020 7370 3503

From the Editors

We're now comfortably settled at our new home in Hoxton Square which, being a proper office rather than part of a flat, is far more spacious and functional than Brewhouse Yard. We do miss the spectacular view we had there of London's domes and towers rising against the sky behind St Paul's, but we're enjoying the edgy inner city feel of Hoxton with its little specialist bookshops, vegetarian restaurants and bicycles chained to the railings among the plane trees and scruffy city pigeons. Thank you so much, all of you who sent us good wishes for the move and appreciative Christmas cards. We were extremely touched to receive them.

This year certainly feels like a busy one, with various dates already in the diary. On Saturday 23 March Gordon Bowker, biographer of Lawrence Durrell, George Orwell and James Joyce, will be speaking about another of his subjects, Malcolm Lowry (see p.45), as part of the *Slightly Foxed* series of talks on forgotten authors at the Oxford Literary Festival. Tickets from the Festival box office: 0870 343 1001.

On Wednesday 19 June we'll be giving a 'Tea with *Slightly Foxed*' at the Simonsbath Festival on Exmoor to launch the summer issue. It's a wonderful part of the world and the Festival looks like a very interesting and eclectic series of events, from a concert by an all-female trumpet quartet to an evening with Thomas Hardy (www.simonsbathfestival.co.uk). Likewise the Penzance Literary Festival – a charmingly friendly and informal festival in another beautiful place – where we'll be talking about the experience of founding and editing *Slightly Foxed* and hosting tea again in July (www.penzance-literary-festival.org.uk).

We've also booked ourselves in at the Art Workers' Guild in Bloomsbury again for our 2013 Readers' Day which will be on Saturday 9 November. Those who come do seem to love it and tickets go fast, so if you're interested let us know in good time. We do look forward to meeting some of you at these events – it's one of the nicest parts of the job.

The latest of the Slightly Foxed Editions, out this spring, is Ysenda Maxtone Graham's gripping biography of her grandmother, *The Real Mrs Miniver* (see p.12). Those of you who bought and loved her *Mr Tibbits's Catholic School* will know what a sparky writer Ysenda is. In this book she plumbs the experience of another writer, an intriguing woman who found herself caught in a web of her own creation; it's an absolute page-turner.

If you missed out on the Slightly Foxed Editions, two of our best-loved titles are now available as Slightly Foxed paperbacks: Priscilla

Napier's account of growing up in Egypt during the last golden years of the Edwardian Age, *A Late Beginner*, and Michael Jenkins's *A House in Flanders*, his evocation of the magical summer he spent as a shy 14-year-old with 'the aunts in Flanders' – a formative experience he would never forget.

And finally, our best wishes to you all for 2013, and congratulations to Brian Midgley, the winner of our 4th crossword competition, who receives a year's free subscription. The answers appear at the bottom of p.95.

GAIL PIRKIS

HAZEL WOOD

Dreaming of the Bosphorus

ATES ORGA

My father Irfan Orga (1908–70) first set foot in England in July 1942, as a staff captain commanding Turkish Air Force pilots completing their training with the RAF. The posting changed his life. In London, challenging the Turkish law of the day forbidding members of the armed forces or diplomatic service from cohabiting with foreign nationals, he took up with a young, irregularly beautiful Norman-Irish lapsed Catholic, Margaret, then married to someone else. She assumed his surname in 1944, seven months before I was born.

Leaving his desk at the Turkish Embassy, Father returned to Turkey after the war, resigning his commission in January 1946. But his 'crime' rumbled on. Appalled by the possibility of imprisonment, friends in high places and his brother-in-law, one of Atatürk's security chiefs before the war, urged him to leave the country. Given just a one-month visa, he flew to Northolt on 23 December 1947, my mother (and I) following on the 27th. Within a fortnight they were married, 48 hours after her divorce came through, and on 23 February 1948 the Home Office granted him indefinite leave to stay and work in Britain. Nineteen months later a Turkish court found him guilty *in absentia* and placed a fine on his head roughly equivalent to £145,000 today. His appeal against his conviction was unsuccessful and he never went back to Turkey, spending his last days in Kipling country near Tunbridge Wells, victim eventually of depression, loss of self-esteem and a weakened heart.

Irfan Orga, *Portrait of a Turkish Family* (1950, revised ed. 2011)
Eland · Pb · 332pp · £12.99 · ISBN 9780907871828

Initially called *On the Shore of the Bosphorus* and longer than the version we're familiar with today, *Portrait of a Turkish Family*, completed in west London by the summer of 1949, was the first and arguably the finest of my father's nine published books. An autobiography of tears and goodbyes, dedicated to my mother, it reached fruition on a Hermes portable typewriter in a small fourth-floor Bayswater tenement room lit by a naked 40-watt bulb and permeated by the aroma of cheap cigarettes, stale perfume, and Mediterranean beans simmering away slowly somewhere in the basement. My mother was ill with pulmonary tuberculosis, necessitating spells in hospital. During the day, using twigs, I'd play 'boats' in Kensington Gardens. At night, lulled by the click-clack carriage-return of Mother's typing, I'd go to sleep in a corner with my rag-dolls. I remember gas lamps, yellow-grey smog, sleeting rain, dusty summer streets, the pulverized, rusting skeletons of houses with rooms blown apart, coal smoke on the wind, food rationing, steamed-up December windows sealed with newspaper, flour and water. Since Father had no paid employment money was scarce, visits to the pawnbroker were a way of life, and food parcels from Turkey a necessity.

Five, ten years after the war, Bayswater was the haunt of *émigrés* and refugees, prostitutes and fugitives. A place scented by the smells of the East, presided over by the late Edwardian extravagance that was Whiteley's department store. Eventually we moved to the Notting Hill end of Pembridge Square (detached pastel-washed Victoriana, full of old campaigners come home to pasture). Most of my father's later books were written there.

The Round Pond, Peter Pan, the Albert Memorial – the stage of my childhood never changed. It brought stability and continuity to my life, a happy counterpoint to the rigour of daily lessons with my father (I never went to school). My acquaintances and friends came principally from two private Catholic institutions on opposite sides of the park – the girls from Our Lady of Sion (my mother's old convent), the boys from St Philip's ('Dick Tibbits's place'). We enjoyed each other's company, but no one for a moment knew the realities of our household. The Orga family kept its life, troubles and triumphs to itself, Father firmly instilling his grandmother's dictum that you should 'never let anyone know when you are desperate. Put your best clothes on and pride on your face and you can get anything in this world – otherwise you will get nothing but kicks.'

Planned and sketched by my father (writing first in Ottoman Arabic script, then Turkish Latin, then rough English), tidied up and poeticized by my mother on her better days (his story, her stylistic and linguistic brilliance), *Portrait of a Turkish Family* was published by Victor Gollancz in August 1950, Macmillan of New York issuing an Americanized version three months later. Bridging the period from the sunset of the Ottoman Empire to the dawn of the Turkish Republic, from the last sultans to Atatürk, the book tells of a socially well-connected Istanbul family, carpet merchants, who survive war, occupation and disaster but lose everything except their dignity and will to fight another day. The early chapters introduce us to pre-war domestic life within the shadow and call to prayer of the Blue Mosque. 'Amongst my earliest recollections is the soft, unceasing sound of the Marmara and the singing of the birds in the gardens. Our house was a big wooden house, painted white with green shutters and trellised balconies front and rear. It belonged to my grandfather and my grandmother and we lived there with them.' Where the men of the family originated from isn't clear. But at the end of 1914, Turkey having sided with the Kaiser, they marched off to battle – to Gallipoli and the Syrian desert – and never returned.

Their demise left my father's Albanian mother, 13 at the time of his birth, and his Macedonian grandmother to salvage an existence. In a book layered with cameos of a world in meltdown, of a city of wood going up in flames, it is these two women who leap most immediately off the page. The grandmother, the black-clothed, henna-haired 'autocrat at the hamam', doesn't want life or tradition to change. She sits behind latticed windows reading the Koran; she

9

helps herself to Turkish Delight and rose sherbet; she 'screams' orders and 'roars' instructions; 'obstinate, wayward, indomitable,' she quarrels, interferes and criticizes. And remarries.

Contrastingly, my father's mother, Şevkiye, comes over as a gentler soul, a pragmatist who faces up to the present, doesn't take a new husband, and, at 45, ends her life losing her mind in a mental asylum. She's 'slim and haughty with the flaring wing of nose and the delicate eyebrows that seemed painted on'. Scratching a living, she does needlework and embroiders silk with vivid strands of back-lit colour, each design a one-off. She haggles with market-traders and speaks in halting French with her foreign clientele.

As the 'bread-winner' of the family, fighting for three children in a hostile climate, she looks ahead with quiet resolve. She argues for change – and finally rebels. One day in 1918 she throws away her veil, leaving 'her lovely face naked to the world'. To the dismay of the neighbourhood, whose boys stone and jeer her; and the consternation of her mother-in-law, who frets that she'll be seen as a 'tango' or prostitute, 'a fast woman'. Come 1916,

> Food was running short in the whole country. At the [charity] school [in Kadiköy across the water] we had now begun to leave the dining-room hungry after meals, and no more butter appeared on the tables. We went to sleep hungry, awoke hungry and went through the day hungry.

Two years on Irfan and his sick little brother Mehmet returned home – but not joyously. 'Bitterness brooded because one had left this meanness for another kind of meanness and one had returned no better off . . . why had [our mother] . . . banished two small boys to a German-influenced school, killing all trust and love, then trying to win it back when it was too late?'

In May 1919, coincident with the Turkish War of Independence, Irfan, not yet 11, entered Kuleli, the military high school on the Asiatic side of the Bosphorus founded by Abdülmecid I in 1845. The move, orchestrated by Şevkiye, determined his destiny. Palatial Kuleli and its twin turrets, backed by hills and woods, has always been one of the iconic sights of the Bosphorus shoreline, whether in the heat of a turquoise summer day or floodlit at night, a beacon for passing ships. Its presence pervades the second half of the *Portrait*.

The *Portrait* proved such a hit that a second edition had to be rushed through in days. That halcyon summer of 1950 no bookshop in London was without a copy. English luminaries – John Betjeman; Harold Nicolson, a seasoned Turcophile; Peter Quennell, editor of the *Cornhill Magazine* – all were quick to praise, and did so generously. The strength of the narrative lay in its independence, its novelty (mid-twentieth century Western society knew little then about Turkey or Turkish life), and the fact that it stood outside the literary mainstream and had no axe to grind. It read like a novel; painted exotic scenes with the sharpness of a Bartlett engraving or a photograph by Istanbul's chronicler Ara Güler; and unfolded universally experienced feelings of love, deprivation, tragedy, parting and growing up.

Sixty years on, many reprints and translations later, a new generation of readers has taken the book to its heart, while in Turkey it has become required reading. Television serialization beckons.

Portrait of a Turkish Family ends in 1942, in 'the raw chill winter of Anatolia', with my father leaving Ankara, England-bound. 'When I think of you who are gone,' the book finished originally,

> long-dead dreams rise up again to catch me by the throat this last evening . . . All the graceful life you represented comes back in full measure to haunt this jaundiced eye, to torture this foolish heart for the things that might have been had Time stood still . . . 'Good-bye,' we shout. 'Good-bye . . .'

ATES ORGA is a writer and classical recording producer. His books include biographies of Beethoven and Chopin as well as a recent personal anthology of poems, *Istanbul*, in Eland's Poetry of Place series.

Common Sense Dancing

ALLISON PEARSON

She began life as the fictional heroine of a small newspaper column and went on, via American bestsellerdom and a celebrated wartime Hollywood movie, to have the kind of impact on world affairs that solemn male writers can only dream of. Winston Churchill and Eleanor Roosevelt were among her fans. The former claimed she did more for the Allied cause than a flotilla of battleships.

It's true that if you hadn't already come across Caroline Miniver, a happily married, upper-class wife and mother, going about her pre-war round of London dinners and country-house parties, she might sound paralysingly dull and indeed insufferably smug. Mrs Miniver purchases an engagement diary! Mrs Miniver recruits a charlady! Mrs Miniver ponders the acquisition of a new motor car! How trivial and spoilt, you might suppose. And so it could have been, were it not for the remarkable observational gift and radiant humanity of Mrs Miniver's creator, Joyce Maxtone Graham, alias Jan Struther, whose own complicated double life is revealed in *The Real Mrs Miniver*, Ysenda Maxtone Graham's wonderful biography.

Born Joyce Anstruther in 1901, she shared her birth initials with another great English miniaturist, Jane Austen. Famously, Austen described the world of her novels as 'the little bit (two inches wide) of ivory on which I work'. In neither case should narrowness of society be mistaken for smallness of mind or limitation of talent. Both Jane and Joyce could find the universal in a picnic or in the daily doings of well-bred wives who shop at Peter Jones.

It was 1937 when Joyce Anstruther, petite, beady-eyed writer of poems, hymns and comic sketches for *Punch*, was asked by Peter

Fleming, a leader-writer on *The Times*, to help cheer up the paper's Court pages. Fleming wanted to add 'a light and feminine touch', in the form of occasional stories about a fictional woman. 'What sort of woman?' Joyce asked. 'Oh, I don't know – just an ordinary sort of woman who leads an ordinary sort of life. Rather like yourself.'

The Mrs Miniver pieces appeared every fortnight for two years and were collected in book form in October 1939. They were signed simply 'from a correspondent', though, as Ysenda Maxtone Graham remarks in her prologue to *The Real Mrs Miniver*, 'There seemed no doubt that they must have been written by a contented, well-balanced, happily married woman who longed to share her joy in life, and her peace of mind, with *Times* readers.'

As Joyce Anstruther's granddaughter, Ysenda knew how far from the truth that picture was. Joyce/Jan was a cat's cradle of contradictions. A woman who wrote simple, rapturous hymns, like 'Lord of All Hopefulness', she was a complicated agnostic. Author of a stirring, patriotic portrait of Blighty hailed as a wartime classic, she left London for America in 1940 and was accused of both hypocrisy and treachery. Born into a grand family (she attended school with the future Queen Mother), throughout her life the 'raggle-taggle gypsy in her head' dared her to run off and do something wild. A sociable creature with a contagious zest for life, she struggled with vile depressions which she called 'the Jungles'. Even as she was writing about Mrs Miniver's blessed, enviable marriage to Clem, a successful architect, her own once happy union with Anthony (Tony) Maxtone Graham, a Lloyd's broker, was in trouble beyond repair.

In real life, the writer whose fictional heroine delighted readers with her fortitude and loyalty had begun an affair with a penniless Viennese Jewish poet and refugee called Adolf ('Dolf') Placzek. While Joyce was touring the US wearing her Mrs Miniver hat, giving uplifting speeches to crowds of rapt Americans, she was also meeting her lover for passionate trysts. 'No one guessed – no one could possibly have guessed – that she was living two parallel lives,'

Dolf and Joyce in Brighton, 1940

writes Ysenda Maxtone Graham.

In lesser or more salacious hands, this biography could so easily have been one of those lip-smacking tabloid-style exposés: 'Revealed: The Dark Truth about the Saintly Mrs Miniver!' It is Jan Struther's good luck – and ours – that the author of *The Real Mrs Miniver* is not just her own granddaughter, with all the familial concern that implies, but also the inheritor of her remarkable talent.

I think it was Clive James who said that humour is 'common sense dancing'. That will do perfectly for both Ysenda and the grandmother who tragically died aged 52 in 1953, nine years before Ysenda was born. Both writers can make thoughts and feelings dance on the page, not just for effect – though the effect is often lovely – but the better to make us understand what it's like to live inside another human being's head. Here is Ysenda, scalpel in hand, with her grandparents' dead marriage on the slab, trying to dissect what went wrong: 'There came a time when Tony was only comfortable when he was inside the safe walls of an anecdote, with its beginning, middle and end.'

That is every bit as good a skewering of middle-aged male withdrawal into life's golf club as Joyce Anstruther's own reflections on 'the genus Old Boy'. Both magpies with an ability to 'pick out lovely bits suddenly', Joyce and Ysenda can be ruthless when it comes to setting down the truth. 'If she was not enjoying something, she liked to ruin it for everyone else,' concludes Ysenda briskly, when describing a holiday Joyce took with friends.

The grandmother who deplored the fact that most adults so outgrow their childhood selves that they become 'great big f***ing bores' might well have winced at some of Ysenda's observations, but the writer in her would surely have applauded the lethal, epigrammatic summing-up of Joyce as a mother: 'The love she felt for her children was all the more intense because she saw so little of them.'

Throughout the book, Ysenda's method is gently to peel apart Joyce's double life by juxtaposing her published prose and poetry with private diaries, letters and the recollections of friends and relatives. She quotes at length from the miraculously good 'Christmas Stockings' piece. In it, Mrs Miniver reflects how the tender pleasures of early morning on 25 December can, at a stroke,

> pay off the accumulation on the debit side of parenthood – the morning sickness and the quite astonishing pain, the pram in the passage . . . the pungent white mice, the shrivelled caterpillars; the nameless horrors down the crevices of armchairs; the alarms and emergencies, the swallowed button, the inexplicable earache, the ominous rash appearing on the eve of a journey; the school bills . . . the emotional compromises, the divided loyalties, the adventures continually forsworn.

After letting the passage work its magic, Ysenda adds quietly that, in her annotated copy of *Mrs Miniver*, Joyce's daughter Janet had scribbled, 'I don't remember my parents forswearing many adventures.'

This is the best kind of biographical sleuthery: entering without breaking. Ysenda doesn't cry 'Gotcha!' at this discrepancy between the selfless ideal committed to print by Joyce, and the reality of frequently absent parents which her daughter later recalled. She is subtle enough to appreciate that her grandmother was not lying; what she set down was both true and untrue in the way that fiction always is. That writers are shits and angels, that out of 'frivolity and unbelief' can come hymns which shore up people's faith, just as out of attention-seeking and black mood-swings can come the sweet consolation and eternal wisdom of Mrs Miniver.

Am I making the book sound too bleak? Lord, I hope not. Yes, it is shot through with sadness, but there are only a handful of mortals who have been fully alive to what the poet Louis MacNeice called 'the drunkenness of things being various' and Joyce Anstruther was one of them. Her granddaughter captures that intoxication in this biography. In 1939, just after they met, Joyce and Dolf went to one of Myra Hess's famous wartime piano recitals at the National Gallery. Afterwards, on the steps outside, Ysenda tells us that her tiny grandmother looked up at the lofty Dolf and said: 'Bach is so all-right-making, isn't he?'

Mrs Miniver – the Hollywood version

'Who is this magical creature who can express what I have always thought about Bach, but have never found the right words?' thought Dolf.

The Real Mrs Miniver is very all-right-making. In 2002, it was shortlisted for the Whitbread Biography of the Year, though I can't think of a more deserving winner. In the past decade, I must have given it as a gift to everyone I love, because it is about love and, like all the best books, it teaches us how to live.

Towards the end of her too-brief life, Joyce Anstruther drew up a characteristically brave, funny, defiant list which outlined the conflicts of a double life in which she had often been mistaken for her own fictional heroine. The first persona she described as follows: 'Jan Struther, the well-known and successful writer, lecturer, radio-performer etc (with a subdivision called Jan Struther, the much-too-little-known and really pretty terrific serious poet whose depth and brilliance will only really be appreciated by a discerning literary public after she is dead).'

What Joyce couldn't know was that, nine years after she died, a girl would be born who would grow up and use that same really pretty terrific gift to bring her grandmother back to life.

ALLISON PEARSON is a columnist for the *Daily Telegraph* and has written two novels.

Ysenda Maxtone Graham's *The Real Mrs Miniver* (320pp) is now available from *Slightly Foxed* in a new limited and numbered cloth-bound pocket edition of 2,000 copies, each priced at £16 (UK), £18 (Europe) or £19 (Rest of the World). All prices include post and packing. Copies may be ordered by post (53 Hoxton Square, London N1 6PB), by phone (020 7033 0258) or via our website www.foxedquarterly.com.

The following Slightly Foxed Editions are still available:

James Lees-Milne, *Another Self*
Ted Walker, *The High Path*
Graham Greene, *A Sort of Life*
Edward Ardizzone, *The Young Ardizzone*
P. Y. Betts, *People Who Say Goodbye*
Frances Wood, *Hand-grenade Practice in Peking*
Dodie Smith, *Look Back with Love*
Suzanne St Albans, *Mango and Mimosa*
Elspeth Huxley, *The Flame Trees of Thika*
Alan Moorehead, *A Late Education*
Denis Constanduros, *My Grandfather* & *Father, Dear Father*

The Sound of Youth

WILLIAM PALMER

The music that accompanies our youth and first loves remains with us all our lives. It may not be the greatest music, but it is the first and is anchored in our hearts.

It's odd to recall that until the rock and pop revolution of the early Sixties, most British towns had at least one band, usually consisting of a trumpet and trombone, drummer, bass player and out-of-tune pianist thumping out rough versions of New Orleans and Dixieland jazz to young audiences in the back rooms of pubs. This was good drinking and jiving music, although as a young smart alec in those days I snobbishly preferred modern jazz. However, in no forms of jazz did I ever see anyone playing the bass saxophone, the instrument celebrated in Josef Škvorecký's wonderful novella *The Bass Saxophone*.

The bass saxophone is so large that it has to be played standing up, or tilted sideways if sitting. (There is actually an even larger saxophone, the 7-foot-high contra-bass, which looks like the heart of a Gothic plumbing system and gives out what can most politely be described as a series of deep gastric rumbles.) Only one man ever produced good jazz on the bass sax, and that was the American Adrian Rollini in the 1930s (he also mastered something called 'the hot fountain pen').

Josef Škvorecký, *The Cowards* (1958) · Penguin · Pb · 416pp · £9.99 · ISBN 9780141047676; *The Bass Saxophone* (1967) · Ecco Press · Pb · 216pp · $12.95 · ISBN 9780880013703. *The Swell Season* (1975) is out of print.

Rollini is mentioned in *The Bass Saxophone*, and the instrument itself acts as a gigantic and glowing symbol of the freedom and individualism that Škvorecký found in jazz; what he calls 'an *élan vital*, a forceful vitality, an explosive creative energy' in his autobiographical introduction to the novel. And when we know something of Škvorecký's life we can see that the romantic, naïve 18-year-old who narrates the story is his alter ego.

Josef Škvorecký was born in 1924 in Nachod, Anna Trench in the region of Bohemia, Czechoslovakia. He has described his reaction to the first jazz record he ever heard:

> that terribly scratchy Brunswick seventy-eight spinning on a wind-up phonograph, with the almost illegible label 'I've Got a Guy', Chick Webb and His Orchestra with Vocal Chorus . . . we had no way of knowing this was the great, then seventeen-year-old Ella Fitzgerald. But the message of her voice, the call of the saxes . . . they all came across. Nothing could ever silence them in our hearts.

There were certainly those who tried to silence them. Škvorecký's youth coincided with the Nazi occupation of Czechoslovakia from 1939 to 1945. There was not much doubt as to the Nazis' view of jazz – many of its tunes were by Jewish Americans and its finest instrumental exponents were black Americans. Instructions were issued to all dance orchestras that their playing must be 'commensurate with the Aryan sense of discipline. On no account will Negroid excesses in tempo (so-called hot jazz) . . . be tolerated.' The swing band in which Škvorecký played had to disguise its sheet music as Czech folk tunes, and a watch was kept from the taverns where they played. If a German hove into sight, the band would slip smoothly into a sweet Viennese waltz.

The Bass Saxophone opens quite magically at dusk, when the light

forms 'a puddle of honey'. We are in a small town in Bohemia, occu-
pied by the Germans and inhabited by their enemies and a few
collaborators. The unnamed young man telling us the story is standing in front of the town's hotel when a small grey bus draws up. An
old man pulls out an enormous case. It drops to the ground and
opens a crack so that the evening sun glints 'on the immense, incredible bell of a bass saxophone, as big around as a washbasin'.

On the side of the bus are the words *Lothar Kinze Mit Seinem
Unterhaltungsorchester* – a German entertainment band, certainly not
a jazz band. But the young man is transfixed by the sight of this
instrument. The old man cannot manage the case and asks for help
to carry it inside. There is a difficulty. Much as our hero would like
to touch the instrument, the hotel is for Germans only and across the
square a local, Mr Kana, is watching the two men. The last thing the
young man wants to be taken for is a collaborator. His dilemma is
resolved when a German soldier roughly tells him to help the old
man and he staggers into the hotel with the case.

Up two flights of stairs they stop at room 12A and, as they enter, he
sees a man asleep on the bed. The old man invites him to look at the
saxophone, even try it out if he wants to. He leaves him alone with the
sleeping man and the instrument. From the next room the young man
can hear the hectoring voice of Kühl, a German officer of whom he
has run foul when playing jazz records in the local cinema.

What follows can only be described as a semi-erotic embrace of
young man and saxophone. The parts lie in the case and he lifts the
main body out of its plush bed.

> Then the second part: I put them together. I embraced the
> body with gentle fingers . . . I could not resist . . . I just stood
> there with the mouthpiece in my mouth, my fingers spread and
> embracing the immense body, my eyes misty . . . I had never
> held one before: I felt as if I were embracing a mistress.

And he thinks of the two girls that he is in love with but who (so far) have not succumbed to his advances. Inevitably he has to play the instrument.

I blew into the mouthpiece, running my fingers down the valves; what emerged from the bell . . . was a cruel, beautiful, infinitely sad sound.

The man on the bed does not wake, but the single note, reverberating through the hotel, summons a memorable, not to say grotesque crew to room 12A. A 'haggard little fat man' is followed by an elderly woman with a bulbous nose and bloated body, then a good-looking man with the head of a Roman emperor but with no legs below his knees, then a blonde and very beautiful girl, who looks odd by virtue of her relative normality, then a one-eyed giant leading a hunchback with black glasses on his nose.

The little fat man bows and introduces himself – he is Lothar Kinze – and his orchestra: in order of appearance in the room, they are the leader and violinist, pianist, trumpeter, singer, accordionist and drummer. The man drunkenly asleep on the bed is the bass saxophone player.

Sadly and comically the band tell him tales of their past before the war, recalling days of love in this time of hate, and good food and wine in a world of rationing and ersatz substitutes. None of them is a Nazi; the band is their refuge from the horrors of war, a band 'possible only in wartime, dragging its weepy and incomprehensible message from the glories of one ornate municipal hall to the next, in distant towns on the periphery of battlefields'.

They need a saxophone player. The band cannot go on stage without one. The young man agrees, trying to hide his obsessive desire to play this rarest of jazz instruments. So that none of the local collaborators in the audience will recognize him he is disguised with a ludicrous Groucho Marx moustache and thick eyebrows. In one chilling passage amid the comedy he looks through a peep-hole at the audience of occupying Germans and their wives and sees: 'A velvet gown; and behind it other satined and brocaded German ladies with a mobile jewellery exhibition . . . little shining stories ending in death.' They are wearing the jewels looted from deported Jews.

The audience laps up Lothar Kinze's syrupy sentimentalism and lumpy village dance rhythms. And our hero joins in, losing himself in the ecstasy of playing the great melancholy instrument, despite the deplorable music they are playing. But then, at the end of a number, the band's own bass saxophone player, now awake, plucks him off the stage, takes his place and plays a thunderous jazz solo. The audience is appalled. The evening disintegrates and the young man flees the theatre. Luckily he gets away. In the morning there is no sign of the grey bus or the band: it is as if they were parts of a dream that has dissolved.

The Bass Saxophone is an ecstatic hymn to freedom, rich with the stolen victories of the tyrannized. Škvorecký stayed in Czechoslovakia until 1968 but left when the Russians invaded. He has lived in Canada since then and has written many novels and other works, but it is the studies of the enchantment of youth and young love in the midst of the horrors of the war and the grinding misery and cultural wasteland of the Communist dictatorship that followed, to which I return. The mixed fortunes of his jazz-playing hero can be followed in the novel *The Cowards* and in a wonderful collection of stories, *The Swell Season*. There is a sweetness and an innocence about the would-be knowingness of his very young men, their forbidden music and their innocent and tantalizing girlfriends that are quite unlike anything else in twentieth-century literature.

WILLIAM PALMER's new novel, *The Devil Is White*, has just been published. His *The India House* (2005) is still in print and awaiting eager buyers.

A World of Words

ANNABEL WALKER

Whether by luck or judgement I don't now remember, but I first came across the work of Amos Oz in 1984. The occasion was my sole visit to Israel, when I needed a contemporary guide, my only other literary encounter with Jewish culture having been three historical novels by Isaac Bashevis Singer. Somewhere between Singer's nineteenth-century Poland and Oz's modern stories came the horrors of the Nazi era: the bit of Jewish history that everyone knows and that is built into everyone's idea of the state of Israel. It was in my mind at the time, not least because the parents of our Israeli friend bore the tattoos of the concentration camp on their forearms.

The book that spans the period and would have explained a lot had not yet been written. Amos Oz's memoir of his childhood, youth and family history, *A Tale of Love and Darkness*, was published much later, in 2003. Like all his books it was written in Hebrew – a language that was dead for many centuries before being revived so that immigrants arriving in Palestine from the diaspora could communicate with one another. Oz has described in interviews the extraordinary transformation of 'prayer-book Hebrew' into a 'volcanic' language, one that is 'happening' all the time, and has likened the use of it to playing a musical instrument. Translating it successfully into English must be a formidable challenge but Nicholas de Lange, who has worked closely with Oz for four decades, vividly

Amos Oz, *A Tale of Love and Darkness* (English edition 2004) · Trans. Nicholas de Lange
Vintage · Pb · 528pp · £9.99 · ISBN 9780099450030

conveys the voices not only of the author but also of the crowd of characters who people his pages.

Voices are my abiding memory of *A Tale of Love and Darkness*. The young Amos Klausner (he changed his name to Oz later) was surrounded by people in the densely populated quarter of Jerusalem where he lived for the first fifteen years of his life. Every one of them had an opinion on everything from international politics to the ethical dilemma inherent in buying Arab cheese. And they were eager to share their opinions, occasionally crowding into the Klausners' claustrophobic little flat in order to do so. Oz evokes in intense and by turns hilarious detail the patterns of speech, the preoccupations, fears and prejudices of a community in voluntary exile from everything it holds dear back home in Europe, 'that wonderful, murderous continent':

> On my parents' scale of values, the more western something was the more cultured it was considered . . . Europe for them was a forbidden promised land, a yearned-for landscape of belfries and squares paved with ancient flagstones, of trams and bridges and church spires, remote villages, spa towns, forests and snow-covered meadows.
>
> Words like 'cottage', 'meadow' or 'goose-girl' excited and seduced me all through my childhood. They had a sensual aroma of a genuine, cosy world, far from the dusty tin roofs, the urban wasteland of scrap iron and thistles, the parched hillsides of our Jerusalem, suffocating under the weight of white-hot summer.

The boy soon develops a sense that the 'world-at-large', as it is always described, is a cultured, sophisticated and exciting place. At the same time, it is frightening and threatening because it doesn't like Jews. Along with the European fairy-tales that his mother tells him come other stories, of his parents' family lives in Poland, Lithuania, Odessa and the Ukraine, and these are peppered with incidents that foreshadow the Holocaust, in which some members of his family perished. He decides that when he grows up, he wants to be a book, because books have a better chance of survival than the humans who write them. He lives in a world of stories, whether oral or printed on the pages of the books that line the walls and windowsills of every room in the flat, and the contrast between these and the impoverished life of the dusty streets outside convinces him that 'the whole of reality was just a vain attempt to imitate the world of words'.

Instead, he grows up to understand that the world of words and the whole of reality can be one and the same, and he becomes a writer who can light up page after page with his descriptions of 'reality' in all its detail: from the act of putting his baby foot into his first ever shoe to the ritual of accompanying his parents to a café to meet their 'valuable acquaintances'. He sees the humour and the pathos in everyday events and can reproduce a conversation so vibrantly that you feel you are personally involved. Some of his best portraits are of his grandparents: Grandma Shlomit, who fears the germs of the Levant so violently that she sprays her flat with DDT and blocks the overflow holes of the basins with soap, 'in case the enemy attempted to infiltrate that way'; and her husband Grandpa Alexander, dapper and resolutely optimistic, who blossoms after her death in the company of 'a bevy of well-preserved women in their fifties or sixties' who, his grandson realizes, were attracted to Alexander because he 'loved to understand . . . loved to give himself . . . he loved setting sail, he was never in a hurry to cast anchor'.

Oz was the only child of parents whose university educations had equipped them for a life that, in their new home in the Middle East, was beyond their reach:

In a Jerusalem that was full of immigrants from Poland and Russia and refugees from Hitler, among them distinguished luminaries from famous universities, there were more lecturers and scholars than students.

Oz's father, who knew a dozen languages ancient and modern, spent most of his working life as a librarian in the newspaper department of the National Library. At home, in a cramped flat overflowing with books and thwarted hopes, he instructed his son on everything from the order of the planets to the correct way to file book titles. That son grew up to be such a successful writer that he has been offered several professorships despite the fact that he has, he declares, 'never had any talent for research'. The sad truth is, 'My father's little finger was more professorial than a dozen "parachuted in" professors like me.'

> My father was a cultivated, well-mannered librarian, severe yet also rather shy, who wore a tie, round glasses, and a somewhat threadbare jacket, who bowed before his superiors, leaped to open doors for ladies, insisted firmly on his few rights, enthusiastically cited lines of poetry in ten languages, endeavoured always to be pleasant and amusing, and endlessly repeated the same repertoire of jokes (which he referred to as 'anecdotes' or 'pleasantries').

While Oz's parents lavished attention and instruction on their son, their articulacy faltered in the face of intimacy. They and their friends 'were capable of conversing for hours on end in excited tones about Nietzsche, Stalin, Freud, Jabotinsky, giving it everything they had, shedding tears of pathos, arguing in a singsong, about colonialism, anti-Semitism, justice, the "agrarian question", the "Question of Women", "art versus life", but the moment they tried to give voice to a private feeling what came out was something tense, dry, even frightened, the result of generation upon generation of repression and negation'.

Not only were they constrained by bourgeois European manners and a religious upbringing, they were also hindered by 'a great lack of words'. His parents spoke several languages fluently but used only Hebrew with Amos, and Hebrew had not developed sufficiently to be a language of intimacy. 'Even people like my parents who knew Hebrew well were not entirely its masters. They spoke it with a kind of obsession for accuracy. They frequently changed their minds, and reformulated something they had just said.'

The stories of all these people – neighbours, relations, acquaintances and also writers and politicians – run like threads through this tight-packed memoir. Oz's mother is simultaneously the brightest and the darkest of these threads, committing suicide when he was 12. She was beautiful, intelligent and captivating, a creative romantic unable to come to terms with the limitations of her life. Her loss is alluded to at intervals and interspersed among other recollections, defying chronological order as it colours each memory. Here, for example, he recalls his boyish ambition of becoming a fireman:

But who was it that through most of my childhood I rescued in my fantasies over and over again from the fiery furnace and whose love I earned in return? Perhaps that is not the right way to ask the question, but rather: What terrible, incredible premonition came to the arrogant heart of that foolish, dreamy child and hinted to him, without revealing the outcome, signalled to him without giving him any chance to interpret, while there was still time, the veiled hint of what was going to happen to his mother one winter's evening?

It seems that writing this book was as much an effort on Oz's part to understand what happened to his mother as to commit to paper the memories of his early life. But don't imagine, therefore, that it is a sorrowful tale. It has its tragedies, but many comedies too. It is an absorbing, life-affirming story that he tells, as well as a fascinating insight into the life of Jerusalem during the last years of the British Mandate in Palestine and the creation of the modern state of Israel. Perhaps Amos Klausner did, after all, grow up to be a book.

ANNABEL WALKER writes intermittently from a shed on Dartmoor.

Pillow Talk

OLIVER PRITCHETT *shares some thoughts on the do's and don'ts of reading in bed before he turns out the light.*

The etiquette of bedtime reading is such a delicate matter that we must approach it on tiptoe. In fact, before we get to the bed, let us pause and consider the bedside table – or, more accurately, the pile of books on the bedside table.

Our current reading is on the top of the pile, but in the layers below we can find a display of our good intentions: books we have resolved to finish one day. Some of these may even have been there for years, some perhaps were on the Booker Prize shortlist in 2002. One may be there because of a distant New Year resolution to try Turgenev, say. Another may have been borrowed a shamingly long time ago.

There are also some permanent fixtures in this pile, like the incomprehensible instruction manual for the bedside digital clock radio and also a volume on folkloric ways of predicting the weather and a copy of *Weirdest Proverbs from Around the World* – both presents from distant relations at far-off Christmases.

Rule number one about this pile is: don't show off. Don't leave some dauntingly impressive work on the top just to impress some guest who may stray into the bedroom to leave a coat or to find a paracetamol.

Rule number two: don't leave an unfinished book on the bedside table for more than six months. Put it back on the shelves and try again in three months' time.

While we are here at the bedside table, I'd like to say something about the bedside light, which is fundamental to any discussion of bedtime-reading etiquette. The arrival of the compulsory low energy light bulb has had a profound effect on the way we read in bed. At first it led to a mass outbreak of restlessness and lampshade tilting and then to the realization that the rule book had to be rewritten. What are the proprieties of reading in inadequate light? Two simple rules to start with: the first is that it is not good form to attempt to read your hardback by the light of your partner's iPad. The second is that if you choose to wear a head torch or to use one of those neat little lights that clip on to the book itself it can appear unfriendly and you should remember that reading in bed is best when it is a companionable experience and a shared pleasure.

There is, however, a limit to how much pleasure you can share. Try to avoid reading aloud so many passages from your book that you ruin

it for your partner when he or she has a turn at reading it; avoid reading out a witty phrase or a telling observation if it means you will have to take fifteen minutes to set the scene with an explanation of the plot and description of the characters involved. When reading Dickens (say *Pickwick Papers*) aloud in bed, do not, *on any account*, attempt to do all the voices.

Daniel Macklin

Chuckling is acceptable, provided it is not excessive, and it is a sign of good breeding to explain – as briefly as possible – what is amusing you.

The crucial issue in a bedtime-reading partnership is timing – that is the timing of switching out the light. You know what can happen – just as Phoebe, the long-lost daughter of Lord and Lady Hardcover is about to the reveal the appalling secret of Tome Hall, and as the dashing Octavo Quarto is pulling up his horse in the village of Little Binding, after galloping all night through a thunderstorm to prevent the marriage of Emily Endpaper to the unscrupulous Count Festschrift, and exactly at the moment when Mrs Verso is on the point of realizing that the letter from her Australian godson Jason Index is a clever forgery . . . *click* . . . your partner switches out the light.

What is the best way of deciding when the lights go out? A simple rule is to say that the person reading the most serious book has the final say. So, for example, Gabriel García Márquez trumps P. G. Wodehouse and Mrs Gaskell overrules Jeffrey Archer.

Great dangers lurk behind those words, 'Just let me get to the end of this chapter.' Sometimes 'this chapter' is the early part of the memoirs of a politician and deals with his childhood (with detailed information about how his nanny was a great influence), takes in his schooldays (and extremely long school holidays), includes his time at Oxford and the friends he made (a great deal of name-dropping here), and goes on to describe a period of agonized indecision before he took the plunge into politics because he wanted to change the world for the better. By the time we have reached this point in his life the birds are beginning to clear their throats for the dawn chorus.

I suppose it might be possible to agree, in advance, on the time when the lights will go out, but it's unlikely that both of you will stick to the deadline. There is another complication if your bedtime reading partner is a 'slammer' – this is someone who very suddenly and decisively slams the book shut and, in one movement, switches off the bedside light, turns over and lurches sideways in the bed, grabbing an extra armful of duvet, and crashes off to sleep.

The best defence against a slammer is to make sure your bedside reading is a book with short chapters (Michael Frayn's wonderful *Skios*, for example), or a collection of (non-epic) poems, or a volume of pithy letters. Somebody once said – and I think it was me, actually – the secret of a happy marriage is a good bookmark.

It can never be considered civilized behaviour to engage in competitive bedtime reading – seeing who can get through the most pages, giving frequent sideways glances to keep score and turning pages with a little too much eagerness. There is also a condition known as competitive insomnia; this is a tendency among some couples for both partners to claim to be the worst sleeper. This can lead to the use of underhand tactics, such as switching on the light at

2.30 a.m. to read another chapter of *Middlemarch*. These contests should be stopped before they get out of hand and somebody reaches for Gibbon's *Decline and Fall*. Of course, switching on the light in the early hours to read a few more pages is acceptable within reason and can be a tactful way of indicating to your partner that he – or, perish the thought, she – is snoring.

Surely nobody needs reminding that only a cad reads the newspaper in bed, except first thing in the morning.

There has been endless debate about the optimum number of pillows required for two people reading in bed. Various formulae have been devised, taking into account the temperature of the room, the weight of the books being read, size of print and angle of bedside light. A simple rule of thumb is that a total of eight pillows is just about adequate and thirteen is getting close to being excessive. As for the way the pillows are shared out, clearly the person with the thickest volume is entitled to the fattest ones – and the most.

Sometimes I have done without pillows altogether and tried reading while lying flat on my back. This can be dangerous and is not to be recommended with a heavy volume. So, it's well worth remembering, uneasy lies the head that reads *Wolf Hall* in bed.

In bed, OLIVER PRITCHETT prefers a hard mattress and a hard pillow to go with his hardback of Dickens's *Hard Times*.

Map Magic

C. J. SCHÜLER

When I worked on a national newspaper, an old, battered copy of *The Times Atlas of the World* stood propped against the Comment desk. The red cloth binding had come off and the signatures had fallen apart, like breakaway provinces seceding from a crumbling empire. As various benighted places – Darfur, Basra, Helmand – were thrust into the headlines, our reporters and subs would make off with the relevant pages. This battered relic featured countries that no longer existed: Czechoslovakia, the German Democratic Republic, Yugoslavia and, sprawling across a third of the planet, the Union of Soviet Socialist Republics.

How quickly the world changes, while the atlases on our shelves remain frozen in the geopolitics of the moment at which they were printed. I have at home my mother's old copy of Goodall and Darby's *University Atlas*, published by George Philip in 1948; it is in fact a reprint of a pre-war edition, and across the Baltic republics, in red capitals, the legend INCORPORATED IN RUSSIA AUG 1940 has been overprinted, while a dashed red line divides East Prussia into zones of Russian and Polish occupation as of 1945.

The Russian zone is now the Kaliningrad *oblast*, one of Europe's strangest anomalies: an isolated pocket of Russian territory the size of

The Times Comprehensive Atlas of the World (13th edition, 2011) · Times UK · Hb · 544pp · £150 · ISBN 9780007419135; Nicholas Crane, *Mercator: The Man Who Mapped the Planet* (2003) · Phoenix · Pb · 416pp · £10.99 · ISBN 9780753816929; Michael Swift and Angus Konstam, *Cities of the Renaissance World: Maps from Civitates Orbis Terrarum* (2008), is out of print.

Northern Ireland. Since the collapse of the Soviet Union, it has been separated from the rest of the Russian Federation by Poland and Lithuania. Stranded amid the grim Soviet architecture of its epony-mous capital are a few scant remains of the ancient Prussian city of Königsberg. When I was there a couple of years ago, a Russian, whose grandparents had migrated there from Sverdlovsk, told me: 'History for us began in 1946. We didn't know any of the old names.' Marion Dönhoff, a Prussian countess who escaped the advance of the Red Army on horseback, called one of her volumes of memoirs *Namen die keiner mehr nennt* ('Names no one speaks any more'), lamenting the loss of old place names such as Eydtkuhnen, Palmnicken and Trakehnen – strange, lyrical and archaic, more Baltic than German. (These towns and villages are now Chernyshevskoye, Yantarny and Yasnaya Polyana respectively.)

A still older volume, an 1869 edition of *Philip's Family Atlas* which I found, on the brink of disintegration, in my local south London Oxfam shop and repaired myself, testifies to an earlier and now almost inconceivable political geography: a Turkey in Europe encom-passing Romania, Bulgaria, Serbia, Bosnia and much of Greece; an Austrian Empire stretching from Prague to Venice and from Lemberg (now Lviv in Ukraine) to Dubrovnik; and pre-unification Germany's patchwork quilt of statelets – Anhalt, Brunswick, Hessen-Darmstadt, Sachsen-Coburg, Sachsen-Weimar, Waldeck. Above them looms the mighty Prussia which, just two years after the map was printed, would swallow them all.

Atlases have been a familiar fixture in schools, offices, universities and homes for longer than any of us can remember, but it is worth bearing in mind that 'the atlas' came into being at a specific time and in a specific place. In the course of writing a series of illustrated histories of cartography, I have examined the rich collection of historic atlases in the Royal Geographical Society in London. Inhaling the dust rising from the stiff, creaking pages of these massive leather-bound folios, I was able to trace the birth and evolution of the form.

The progenitor of them all is the *Geographia* of Claudius Ptolemy, a Greek geographer and astronomer working in Alexandria around AD 140. If his survey of the world as known to the ancients contained maps, they did not survive the long process of transcription and translation from Greek into Arabic and then, in the later Middle Ages, from Arabic into Latin. It did, however, contain tables of co-ordinates that allowed Renaissance cartographers to reconstruct his map of the world and the 28 regional maps, from Britain to Sri Lanka, that followed it. The copy in the RGS library was printed by Johannes Reger in Ulm, in 1486, its embossed leather covers fastened by metal clasps. Within, the luminous hand-colouring on its woodcut maps is as fresh as the day it was applied. Inside the front board, a bookplate reads: 'William Morris, Kelmscott House'.

The development of printing greatly facilitated the production and distribution of maps, and the process was accelerated in the mid-sixteenth century as woodcuts were superseded by copperplate engraving, which allowed greater accuracy and longer print runs. An enterprising Venetian publisher, Antonio Lafreri, began to bind maps by a variety of cartographers into folio volumes to the order of his customers; collectors call them IATO, 'Italian, Assembled to Order', atlases.

The first atlas in the modern sense of a book of maps conceived and executed as a unity, however, was the *Theatrum Orbis Terrarum* published by Abraham Ortelius in Antwerp in 1570, which featured an engraving of Atlas, the Titan punished for his rebellion against the Olympians by being condemned to support the weight of the world on his shoulders. (A decade earlier, however, in 1559, William Cunningham's *The Cosmographical Glasse* had depicted Ptolemy as Atlas, supporting an armillary sphere representing not just the Earth but the entire cosmos.)

The word 'atlas' itself was first applied to a collection of maps by Ortelius's friend Gerard Mercator, who in 1569 had devised the cylindrical projection that bears his name and became the definitive

way of looking at the world for the
next 400 years. He published the first
four volumes of his atlas between 1585
and 1589, with a fifth being published
by his son Rumold in 1595. For more
than a century, the Low Countries
would be at the forefront of European
map-making, as a close-knit network
of family businesses in Antwerp and
Amsterdam produced a succession of
ever-more detailed and elaborate maps,
framed with ornate Baroque strap-
work and embellished with ships, sea
monsters and allegorical figures. In 1606

Mercator, from his *Atlas
sive Cosmographicae meditationes de
fabrica mundi*

Jodocus Hondius bought Mercator's plates and reissued his atlas,
adding new maps. After Hondius's death, they were sold to the globe-
and instrument-maker Willem Jansz Blaeu. His son Joan, official car-
tographer of the Dutch East India Company, continued the business,
eventually publishing the family's most celebrated work, the magnifi-
cent *Atlas Maior*, in 1665. This golden age of Dutch cartography only
came to an end in 1672, when a fire at the Blaeu warehouse destroyed
many of the plates.

Why the Netherlands? One reason was that it lay on another of
Europe's geopolitical front lines, racked by a prolonged and bitter
war between the newly independent, and Protestant, United
Provinces in the north and Catholic Spain, which still controlled
what is now Belgium. Hondius's world map *Typus Totius Orbis
Terrarum*, printed in Amsterdam around 1598, makes explicit refer-
ence to the conflict, depicting a Christian knight representing the
French King Henri IV, an ally of the Dutch, fighting the figures
of Vanity, Sin, Carnality, the Devil and Death, symbolizing the
forces of Catholicism. While cartographers living in the crucible of
Europe's religious conflict endured hardship and oppression they

were also able to maintain contacts on both sides of the politico-religious divide and so could draw on the discoveries of the seafarers of Spain, the Dutch East India Company and England, where religious exiles including Hondius and his brother-in-law Pieter van den Keere sought asylum and met Frobisher, Hakluyt and Norden.

Religious wars notwithstanding, the Dutch succeeded in building a mercantile empire that ranged from New Amsterdam (New York) to South Africa and the far-flung islands of Indonesia, from where Abel Tasman charted the shores of Australia and New Zealand. The Low Countries became a cradle of art and science, infused with the humanist ideals of the Renaissance and supported by a flourishing merchant class who could afford to buy atlases and huge wall maps to display both their wealth and their global connections. Cartography was central to the culture: Ortelius was a friend of Pieter Brueghel the Elder, Vermeer's painting *The Geographer* depicts a globe by Hondius and a sea chart by Willem Blaeu, while the marble floor of the Citizens' Hall of the Koninklijk Paleis in Amsterdam is inlaid with maps of the eastern and western hemispheres.

Several years ago, I visited the Plantin-Moretus Museum in Antwerp, where many of these great atlases were printed. It was a winter Sunday, and the city lay under snow. Built around an arcaded courtyard, the fine Baroque house was the home and place of business of the great Renaissance printer Christophe Plantin. His son-in-law Jan Moretus inherited it, and the family firm continued until the nineteenth century when it was finally overtaken by new technology, and the building was donated intact to the state as a museum. Thus, this powerhouse of the north European Renaissance has been preserved exactly as it was. On the ground floor stand the two oldest surviving printing presses in the world, complete sets of dies and matrices and, in the cabinets that line the walls, trays of movable type, some still in its original paper wrapping. Plantin mostly bought fonts from the great typographers of his day such as Garamond, but there is a type foundry here too, and a proof corrector's room, with the desk directly under the window. The library contains not only books printed by Plantin, but also those of his competitors, and some incunabula. A large collection of atlases includes Ortelius's *Theatrum*, the printing of which Plantin took over in 1579. Upstairs in the reception rooms hang 18 portraits commissioned by Balthasar Moretus from Rubens, including a posthumous likeness of Ortelius. As motes dance in the beams of sunlight falling through the leaded, mullioned windows, you feel as if you have indeed stepped into a Vermeer.

Not all the great atlases of the period originated in the Low Countries, however. One of the glories of the RGS collection is a set of Braun and Hogenberg's *Civitates Orbis Terrarum*. As the title suggests, the book, published in Cologne in six volumes between 1572 and 1617, was intended as a companion to Ortelius's *Theatrum Orbis Terrarum*, focusing on cities rather than countries. All the great cities of Renaissance Europe and beyond are shown in plan, as panoramas or, most spectacularly, in 45-degree bird's-eye views that are all the more astonishing because, two centuries before the Montgolfier brothers, such aerial perspectives could only be imagined. Georg Braun, a canon of Cologne Cathedral, compiled the text while Frans Hogenberg assembled the copperplate engravings, many of them based on drawings made on the spot by the artist Joris Hoefnagel. Here is London, 'metropolis of the most fertile kingdom of England', with Old St Paul's and, on the south bank of the Thames, the bear- and bull-baiting rings; here is

Title page from Mercator's *Atlas sive Cosmographicae meditationes de fabrica mundi*

Constantinople, surrounded by shipping in the Golden Horn, the ruins of the Roman hippodrome still visible near Haghia Sophia and the Topkapi Palace; here are Mantua and Marseille, Cairo and Cuzco; and here is Florence, with Brunelleschi's dome, looking much as it does today from the window of a plane coming in to land at the airport.

These atlases enjoyed enormous success all across Europe. 'Methinks it would well please any man', wrote Robert Burton in *The Anatomy of Melancholy*, 'to look upon a Geographical Map, to behold, as it were, all the remote Provinces, Towns, Cities of the World, and never to go forth of the limits of his study, to measure by the scale and compass their extent, distance, examine their site . . . What greater pleasure can there now be than to view those elaborate Maps of Ortelius, Mercator, Hondius &c, to peruse those books of cities, put out by Braunus and Hogenbergius?'

Few modern atlases aspire to the pictorial richness of Braun and Hogenberg, but as you peruse their comparatively sober maps, bear in mind the multiple layers of information – topographic, hydro-graphic, trigonometric, environmental, cultural and political – super-imposed within these sophisticated artefacts. Drawing on millennia of knowledge, from ancient Babylonian astronomers to satellite positioning, they chart our growing understanding of the world we inhabit, and our impact upon it. All human life is here.

C. J. SCHÜLER's *Mapping the World* was published in 2010 and his *Mapping the City* in 2012.

The Wild Ginger Man

ANDREW NIXON

'This', said my father, handing me a battered paperback, 'is the sort of book that people used to hide behind a newspaper when reading it on the train.' I was 16. I took it reverently.

It was a 1967 Corgi edition of *The Ginger Man* by J. P. Donleavy: 'Complete' and, most promisingly, 'Unexpurgated'. Of course I had no inkling then of the tortuous publication saga that lay behind that word 'Unexpurgated'. Nor was I to know that the novel would come to have a profound effect on me – on the way I thought about literature and language, and about human nature in all its secret darkness. I retreated to my bedroom to devour *The Ginger Man*, but by the time I'd reached the first sex scene I'd forgotten that it was supposed to be a dirty book because, like so many readers before me, I had become transfixed by the outrageous charisma of its protagonist, that indelible monster Sebastian Balfe Dangerfield.

Discharged from the US Navy, Dangerfield is studying law at Trinity College, Dublin, class of 1947. He is not a good student. In and out of the city's seediest pubs and vice dens, trading blows and banter with Ireland's craziest drunks, he spends his time raising hell and seducing vulnerable women. 'I'm a man for bedlam,' he declares. His misadventures are frequently hilarious: he flees one bar brawl on an uncontrollable bicycle, starts another dressed as a kangaroo.

Revolving around him is a cast of lunatics and ne'er-do-wells, avant-garde Irish alcoholics and American ex-servicemen hungry for

J. P. Donleavy, *The Ginger Man* (1955)
Abacus · Pb · 352pp · £7.99 · ISBN 9780349108759

civilian action. Everyone is permanently broke. Denied a regular income by his rich father across the Atlantic, Dangerfield survives by sponging off women and running up credit with shopkeepers, all of whom fall for his good looks, charm and Anglicized vowels ('I'm down to my accent,' he observes in a bleak moment). He scurries to the pawnbroker with anything that isn't screwed down and even one thing that is: a mirror in a pub toilet, which he unscrews with a fork. All ill-gotten gains are spent instantly on booze, and so his life ploughs aimlessly on, a blurred carousel of scrounging and starving, fighting and fleeing, in farce and despair.

Given this, *The Ginger Man* might have been a bawdy comic romp, with Sebastian Dangerfield the picaresque anti-hero. But it is not, because something much stranger and darker lies at its heart.

'Mr Dangerfield, would you pass me your plate. Why do you water that little plant in the front with an eye dropper?'

'Miss Frost, you've been spying on me. On me in my secret moments.'

'O I haven't. But why do you do such a funny thing?'

'I'm poisoning the plant.'

'Lord save us.'

'Now look at that plant out there, Miss Frost. Would you say it was much longer for this world?'

'O Mr Dangerfield I don't know what to say. That poor plant.'

'It's something in me, Miss Frost. I thought to myself why don't I slip this plant something to kill it.'

'You don't mean that.'

'I'm a killer.'

Such is Dangerfield's motiveless cruelty. Less amusing is his treatment of his young wife and daughter. Early in the book, a domestic row turns violent:

Marion lunged, her slap landing across his jaw. The child began to scream in the nursery. Sebastian up off the table. He drove his fist into Marion's face. She fell backward against the cupboard. Dishes crashing to the floor. In tattered underwear he stood at the nursery door. He kicked his foot through and tore off the lock to open it. Took the child's pillow from under its head and pressed it hard on the screaming mouth.

There is nothing comic about that incident: it is unforgivable wickedness. Donleavy sacrifices our sympathy for his protagonist early on in the book, yet asks us to stay with him, even laugh with him. And despite ourselves, we do. Why? This is the troubling mystery of *The Ginger Man*.

Over the past half-century a procession of journalists have ventured deep into rural Ireland to track down James Patrick Donleavy. Each paints a similar portrait. Donleavy lives reclusively in a crumbling estate in County Westmeath. Here he has cultivated the persona of an Anglo-Irish country squire: tweedy, formidably bearded and with a bizarre mid-Atlantic accent amalgamating his Bronx upbringing, Irish parentage and pretensions to the English landed gentry.

He combines aristocratic manners with a spiky, almost paranoid combativeness. While serving tea in formal style he tells lurid tales of Dublin in the 1940s when he ran with Brendan Behan, Patrick Kavanagh and other hell-raising artists who provided the models for his characters. Most interviews seem to conclude with him leaping up to demonstrate his boxing prowess. Comical perhaps, but it is this pugnacious streak that enabled Donleavy first to get *The Ginger Man* published, and ultimately to triumph in one of the most bitter and protracted legal battles in literary history.

The Ginger Man was Donleavy's first novel and it took him four arduous years to write. Convinced it was a masterpiece, he was determined not to compromise on material that was, in the 1950s, certain to be banned for obscenity, with the consequence that the final manuscript was rejected by over thirty publishers in Britain and the United States.

Apparent salvation came when Brendan Behan suggested trying the Paris-based Olympia Press, which was already putting out avant-garde literature by Samuel Beckett and Henry Miller and would soon publish *The Naked Lunch* and *Lolita*. Olympia's charismatic owner Maurice Girodias read *The Ginger Man* and agreed to take it on.

The first inkling Donleavy had that something was amiss came when Girodias complained that 'the reader does not become engaged in the book . . . until p.100 or thereabouts'. It was on p.100, Donleavy belatedly noticed, that 'there appeared the first considerable account of a sexual nature'. His suspicions were further aroused when he was required to collect his advance payment in used banknotes from the basement of a seedy Soho bookshop.

Full realization of Girodias's duplicity came when Donleavy received his first printed copy. For Olympia's chief source of income was erotica, and with the authorities breathing down his neck Girodias intended to use *The Ginger Man* to give his business a veneer of literary respectability. To this end he included it in a pornographic series called 'Traveller's Companion', and when Donleavy turned to the back of the volume he saw his precious novel listed alongside such titles as *White Thighs*, *School for Sin* and *The Sexual Life of Robinson Crusoe*. Furthermore, *The Ginger Man* was marked as a 'special volume'. Girodias claimed that this denoted its literary merit but, as Donleavy pointed out, it might also be interpreted to mean that *The Ginger Man* was 'a particularly raunchy variety of dirty book'.

Donleavy vowed revenge. He cut the manuscript to meet British censorship standards and took it to the London publisher Neville Spearman, who published the first British edition in 1956. Girodias retaliated by publishing his own expurgated version with a dust-jacket containing a diatribe against Donleavy, who promptly sued him. And so the tit-for-tat legal battle began, both parties claiming ownership of the publishing rights. Counter-suit followed counter-suit for over twenty years, and the saga was only resolved when Donleavy's wife dramatically bought the Olympia Press from under Girodias's nose at auction. Thus Donleavy found himself in the position of suing himself, and was able to bring the whole sorry business to a close.

In the meantime, the world had changed. Corgi printed the first unexpurgated edition in 1963. It has since sold over 45 million copies worldwide and has never been out of print. Donleavy went on to write a further twelve commercially successful novels, yet what little critical reputation he still enjoys rests almost entirely on *The Ginger Man*. *A Singular Man* and *A Fairy Tale of New York* are fine works, but only Sebastian Dangerfield is indelible.

Critics have puzzled over *The Ginger Man* for years without solving its mystery. In the 1960s Donleavy was grouped with the 'angry young men', but the snobbish Dangerfield couldn't be further from a working-class hero. Reviewers have raved, but about completely different things. Dorothy Parker called *The Ginger Man* 'the picaresque novel to stop them all. Lusty, violent, wildly funny, it is a rigadoon of rascality, a bawled-out comic song of sex.' Conversely, John Banville has praised 'the sense of sweet and delicate melancholy that clings to the pages'.

Lusty and violent, yet sweet and delicate? The answer to the puzzle lies, I believe, in the book's extraordinary style. From the opening sentence ('Today a rare sun of spring.'), the deranged, grammar-mangling prose hops ceaselessly between first and third person, past tense and present. As Donleavy himself has put it: 'I just focused on how to get the words off the page and into the reader's brain, as directly as possible.'

Growl back to sleep. Pull the legs up in the foetal crouch. Marion wearing my underwear. Sometimes the sun would sneak in. Then Marion beating barefoot on the linoleum. Entreaties.

O do get up. In my heart where no one else can hear me, I was saying, now for God's sake, Marion, be a good Britisher and get down there in that little nest of a kitchen and buzz on the coffee like a good girl and would you, while you're at it, kind of brown up a few pieces of bread and I wouldn't mind if maybe there was the suggestion of bacon on it, only a suggestion, and have it all ready on the table and then I'll come down and act the good husband with, ah darling good morning, how are you, you're looking lovely this morning darling and younger every morning. A great one that last. But I come down martyred and mussed, feeble and fussed, heart and soul covered in cement.

Dangerfield's interior monologue is so absorbing that his actions in the physical world appear almost as strange interruptions. He is witty, incisive, delusional, mournful: an all too human mass of contradictions. This is why *The Ginger Man* is simultaneously 'violent' and 'delicate', with a realism that shocks even today.

We know Dangerfield directly, without the interventions of authorial judgement or plot-driven motive, and such intimate knowledge makes it difficult simply to condemn or forgive. This is the mysterious power that has sent generations of journalists deep into rural Ireland, and transfixed 16-year-old boys in their bedrooms.

The final words of *The Ginger Man* are a prayer. At the end of his adventures Sebastian Dangerfield has learnt no lessons and received no comeuppance. It is scandalous, and yet, when I finished the last page of that battered Corgi paperback I could not help but join in – as I still do today – with Donleavy's plaintive plea for

> God's mercy
> On the wild
> Ginger Man.

ANDREW NIXON is the editor of The Dabbler, the culture blog for connoisseurs of everything – www.thedabbler.co.uk.

With a Notebook and a Ukulele

GORDON BOWKER

I first came across Malcolm Lowry through a selection of his poems published in a series devoted mainly to American Beat poets like Allen Ginsberg. But in this slim volume of idiosyncratic verse, every line, every image, spoke of the sea and sailors, of lost horizons, suffering souls and impending madness in a distinctly Anglo-Saxon voice. The words were not those of a rootless New York Beatnik but of a reincarnated Ancient Mariner.

The poetry led me to a collection of Lowry's stories, *Hear Us O Lord from Heaven Thy Dwelling Place*, lyrical meditations on sin and redemption written in British Columbia where he spent fourteen years living in a squatter's shack on the shores of Burrard Inlet. There he also completed his greatest work, *Under the Volcano*, and several novels which remained unpublished during his lifetime. In fact, when he died an alcoholic's death in a quiet Sussex village in 1957 none of his books were in print in English, and his publisher had abandoned him. And yet his writing career had taken off full of promise 24 years earlier with the publication of his first novel, *Ultramarine*.

Lowry was born in 1909, the son of a wealthy Liverpool cotton-broker, and grew up on the Wirral – 'within sight and sound of the

Malcolm Lowry, *Ultramarine* (1933)
Overlook Press · Pb · 204pp · $14.95 · ISBN 9781585676958
Lunar Caustic (published posthumously in 1968) and *Under the Volcano* (1947) are available as Penguin paperbacks (96pp · £3 · ISBN 9780141196114; and 400pp · £9.99 · ISBN 9780141822547).

sea and ships'. His parents, devout Methodists, sent him to the Leys School in Cambridge where he wrote for the school magazine, discovered alcohol and jazz and began composing witty popular songs. A gifted, quirky, eccentric boy who believed that alcohol was a source of creative inspiration, he feared his autocratic father and despised his socially pretentious mother, while they in turn came to fear their increasingly drunken, unpredictable son.

For Lowry the sea represented escape, and a youthful obsession with Conrad, Melville and O'Neill led him to leave school at 17 to sign on as a deck-boy aboard a Liverpool freighter, the SS *Pyrrhus*, trading to the China Seas. His father pulled strings to make this possible on condition that he tried for Cambridge entrance on his return. He set off with a notebook and a ukulele, hoping to collect material for short stories and compose foxtrots during the voyage. Foolishly, in search of publicity, he gave an interview to the *Liverpool Echo* which ran the headline, RICH BOY AS DECKHAND: PREFERS 50S A MONTH TO THE 'SILK-CUSHION LIFE'.

Crew-members, reading this and resenting a public schoolboy going to sea merely 'for experience', while unemployed seamen were left hanging around the dock gates, decided to teach him a lesson.

Throughout the voyage Lowry was picked on and bullied – handed red-hot plates by the cook, smothered with red lead, frog-marched to a Shanghai brothel and jeered at by the crew for being unable to perform in front of them. He returned home vowing to expose his persecutors in a book. This began as a straightforward account of his adventure, drawing on the many notes he had taken: of dockside scenes, names of bars, street signs, advertisements, newspaper headlines, old sailors' stories, poker games and fragments of conversation.

But then a chance discovery transformed the book and the course of his writing career.

Mark Handley

46

He came across Conrad Aiken's *Blue Voyage*, a stream-of-consciousness novel about a transatlantic crossing seen from the viewpoint of a solitary passenger. It was a very literary, self-consciously Joycean novel, and it galvanized young Lowry. Here, he decided, was the style he needed in which to express his own mental suffering at the hands of his heartless crewmates.

In 1929, having gained a place at St Catharine's College, Cambridge, he wrote to Aiken asking to be taught how to write novels; his father would pay. Aiken, an American poet, had been teaching at Harvard but had been dismissed after students complained about the 'immorality' of *Blue Voyage*. Short of funds, he agreed to take on the young Englishman, and Lowry worked his passage across to Cambridge, Massachusetts. There Aiken found himself confronted by a strangely brilliant youth plainly obsessed with him and his work. As an experiment he decided to 'take over' his young admirer and make him an extension of his own consciousness. Aiken, however, was a disturbing influence, unstable and alcoholic, and Lowry returned home strangely possessed by the poet's malevolent spirit and doubly committed to hard drinking.

On the voyage home he discovered Nordahl Grieg's *The Ship Sails On*, another tale of suffering at sea, which gave him a structure and a Norwegian dimension for his own book, now called *Ultramarine*. Up at Cambridge he acquired the reputation of a 'drunken genius', famous for reading passages from his work-in-progress on pub-crawls around the town. Absent-mindedly he would abandon the pages as he read them, and friends would have to tour the city's hostelries next day to retrieve them.

By the time he graduated, *Ultramarine* had evolved into a highly experimental coming-of-age novel following the painful progress of Dana Hilliot, deck-boy aboard the SS *Nawab* (SS *Oedipus Tyrannus* in later editions), as he pines for the girl he has left behind and suffers the spiteful attentions of the crew. It also bears witness to Lowry's breadth of reading, and was, he confessed to Aiken, a patchwork of quotations and allusions to the writers he most admired.

In October 1932, having scraped a pass degree, he went to London, a young author with a book accepted by Chatto for spring publication. Meanwhile, he spent his time carousing around Fitzrovia's pubs at his father's expense with other young literary alcoholics such as Dylan Thomas and John Davenport, adding more tales of prodigious drinking to the Lowry legend.

But for this accident-prone author, catastrophe was never far away. His editor, Ian Parsons, *en route* to Scotland, parked his open-top sports car briefly outside the Chatto office in St Martin's Lane, with Lowry's manuscript in a briefcase on the back seat. When he returned the briefcase had gone. Thinking that Lowry must have a carbon copy, he went on his way and broke the news to the author on his return. To his horror, Lowry had no carbon, having tossed it away when the final draft was typed. If Parsons was dismayed, Lowry was suicidal. He decided to do the rounds of his friends to wish them farewell before killing himself. Fortunately, visiting the old Cambridge crony who had typed the missing manuscript, he found that the carbon copy had been salvaged from the wastepaper-basket into which he had tossed it, and he returned to London in triumph.

Jonathan Cape came up with an improved offer and published *Ultramarine* in June 1933. In *Life and Letters* Hamish Miles called it 'one of the most striking works of imaginative realism that has come my way for a long time'; but V. S. Pritchett in the *New Statesman* thought it 'self-conscious', 'metallic', 'monotonous and unrevealing'. The best review was a short one in the *Illustrated London News* which concluded: 'You look down; the bottom is never reached, but the reflections are fascinating.'

Lowry was deeply depressed by what he saw as a poor reception for the book into which he had poured so much emotional capital over the previous six years. In 1935, having married an American girl, he left for New York, expressing disgust for 'the non-creative bully boys and homosapient schoolmasters of English Literature'.

Ultramarine is a truly poetic novel. Its use of the interior mono-logue invites comparison with Joyce. However, unlike *Ulysses*, which undoubtedly influenced Lowry, it does not attempt to inhabit the consciousness of more than one person but swings from the external life on board the *Nawab* to the elliptical wanderings of Hilliot's con-sciousness through past, present and future around the focal point of a single day on which his innocence is lost. Hilliot is 'a young boy chased by the furies' and 'living in introverted commas', and his fas-cination with the infernal world of the stokehold, where sweating stokers ('flaming nightmares, firelit demons') feed the fires of Hades, adds a Dantesque dimension. For me it is a minor masterpiece, though a flawed one.

Lowry's short stories are probably the best introduction to his work, followed by *Ultramarine*, then *Lunar Caustic*, a brilliant novella set in a New York psychiatric ward. *Under the Volcano* is prob-ably best left till last. The stories, some deceptively simple, offer an easy introduction to Lowry's distinctive world of ideas and allusions; *Ultramarine* and *Lunar Caustic* are literary prologues to *Under the Volcano*, anticipating its greater density and intricate symbolism. In each of these books there is more than one great religious theme – the suffering sinner, the fall of man, the apocalypse, the redemption. Once one has learned to understand Lowry's manner, his strange affinities and way with words, reading his work becomes ever more rewarding. Like Joyce, Lowry is a writer one can either become obsessed with or find unreadable. As a youth I was obsessed; now I am a fond and enduring devotee of someone I consider to be a grossly under-valued but ultimately great English novelist.

GORDON BOWKER's obsession with Lowry led to a biography of the author, *Pursued by Furies*, which appeared in 1993 and was reissued in 2009. He went on to write biographies of Lawrence Durrell (*Through the Dark Labyrinth*, 1996) and George Orwell (2003). His biography of James Joyce was published in 2011.

Putting the Hum into the Humdrum

A.F. HARROLD

I was 5 in 1980 and consequently considered too young to go to London's notorious Comedy Store. But had I stuck on a false beard and got the train up to town I might have seen a 27-year-old ex-bus conductor reading poems about his glasses, his dog and his brother-in-law to a room of angry drunkards who, in those years, dedicated all their hard-earned free time to making comedians cry. I wish I had gone because I would've been the one at the back who got it.

I first encountered John Hegley in the early '90s, though only obliquely, via a schoolfriend who was hipper than me and had one of John's early pamphlets. He showed me a limerick about 'a creature from space/who entered a three-legged race/he was not very fast/in fact he came last/because he was a bag of oven-ready chips'. It may not look like much on the page, but it has three important things going for it: it's silly; it's short; and it makes full use of the last line, adding an extra foot to give the surprise a bigger kick.

There were other poems in there, funny, silly, stupid even. Like 'Grandma's Footsteps':

> Just because she's got a walking frame
> it doesn't mean she's a victim,

John Hegley, *Five Sugars Please* (1993) · Methuen · Pb · 128pp · £7.99 · ISBN 9780413773005; *The Sound of Paint Drying* (2003) · Methuen · Pb · 144pp · £7.99 · ISBN 9780413731807; *Uncut Confetti* (2006) · Methuen · Pb · 128pp · £9.99 · ISBN 9780413775702; *Peace, Love & Potatoes* (2012) · Serpent's Tail · Pb · 120pp · £9.99 · ISBN 9781846688980.

she hangs her budgie on the front,
he's nameless
and she nicked 'im.

Spike Milligan's glorious *Silly Verse for Kids* was a major element of
my youthful reading. In fact I've still got my original copy with its
torn cover and failing binding. That book's mix of Goonish simpli-
city, puckish irreverence and sing-song jingle-like squibs of poems, all
mixed up with Spike's own illustrations, is just the same stuff you
find in Hegley's books.

It was another half dozen years before I finally saw him live and I
wasn't disappointed. To say the man is a good performer is like saying
a potato is edible: it simply doesn't go far enough (a potato being
edible, you see, in so many different ways). John's on-stage manner is
bluff, his demeanour deadpan, bored even (it's often described as
schoolmasterly, and he claims he adopted this in those early Comedy
Store days in an effort to keep crowds controlled), but now and then a
sudden unlikely flash crosses his face and he's grinning, crook-toothed
and childishly joyous, like an infant who's just heard a teacher fart.
Loudly. In an instant he changes from schoolmaster to co-conspirator.

But I'm not going to waste ink on John's stage work: instead I
want to write about how he looks in books. (Which isn't to say that
if he's performing near you you shouldn't go, because you should.)

Unlike the other performance poets of that alternative comedy
surge, John seems actually to like poetry for poetry's sake. His isn't an
angry voice, he hasn't a political axe to grind. Open his books and
you find the absurd cuddled up side by side with family life. Tales of
his beloved glasses and his antipathy to contact lenses ('I don't like
contact lenses/and can you wonder why/if you want to put one
in/you have to poke yourself in the eye'), rub along with regular
canine eulogies ('my doggie don't wear glasses/so they're lying when
they say /a dog looks like its owner/aren't they') and stories of John's
childhood in Luton.

The Beatles in Our Luton Bungalow

With the Beatles about
you had to admit
that it got better.
They put a hum
into the humdrum
and the drab.
Those four made us glad to be alive.
They made the five of us feel fab.
They were one of the three things
our family could appreciate together.
The other two were sleep
and oxygen.

Whatever story Hegley is telling, it's the language, and the crystal-clear joy he takes in it, that sets him apart: the poems are almost as much there for the sound of the words he's found as they are for the joke he's telling. His rhythms and rhymes, his timing and the way lines stretch to fit the rhyme in, are a delight.

This is something you notice on stage or in conversation with him: it's the mistake, the verbal slip or trip that whips a flurry of sparks in the dark of his brain, linking words and sounds nonsensically to see if sense can be teased from the vocabularial cracks. It's a linguistic tic, his love of words, the way they spill out.

The Happy Mistake

One night I heard another poet say
'omelette'
when he meant to say
'Hamlet'.
I wish him well with his gift.

In his 1993 collection *Five Sugars Please*, there's a prose piece called 'The Common Poetry' which describes someone who takes a flyer for his Edinburgh show and gives it back, saying: 'I thought this was a comedy show. Poetry! Stuff that for a game of soldiers.' Hegley then unpacks the phrase, trying to pry into its meaning: is he saying he's 'above playing with little plastic men', or does he mean 'real soldiers and not wanting to risk getting your head blown off?' He concludes that the phrase means neither and both, that it's a compound image, heightened language, ergo, poetry.

Anna Trench

So ironically the man in the queue was actually using poetry to say poetry wasn't for him . . . There is a common poetry which certain poets are committed to enriching, stocking its pool with ever more dazzling word fish. The common poetry abounds; rhyming slang, bingo calls, the names given to race-horses, which are incidentally considerably more imaginative than those given to dogs.

But it's when Hegley turns this poetic ear to face the inner eye and describe the tricky relationship he had with his dad (who was half French) that the poems and the art reach above Milliganish absurdity and achieve what is missing from so much comic verse: a solid, beating emotional core.

> The picture I usually paint of my father
> is the one of him smacking me as a lad:
> hard and uncompromising.
> It is not a lie but neither is it the only angle
> from which one can capture his portrait.

In the title piece of his book *The Sound of Paint Drying* (2003), he makes a journey to France to paint his own version of a painting his

dad (long dead by now, and finally forgiven) had done seventy years
before. He finds the café in his dad's painting, sets up his own easel
and has a go. The story is told simply in prose and snatches of poetry.

> We find my father sat in Nice
> when he was twenty-six,
> he's poking at some canvas
> with his range of hairy sticks.
>
> . . .
>
> And it's highly naturalistic,
> it is not impressionistic
> it is not expressionistic
> neither futurist nor fauve
> it isn't pointillistic,
> it is highly naturalistic,
> in places it is orange
> and in others it is mauve.

The Sound of Paint Drying, besides being a book, was one of the
most compelling half hours of Radio 4 I've heard. John and a tape-
recorder on a quest in France painting a painting, and talking with
his dad who wasn't there. At one point he just lets the microphone
run, while he goes and has a kick-about up the road with some kids.
The finest dead air the radio's heard.

As time has gone on, on stage and in the books, John's mum and
dad and his Luton upbringing, and, subsequently, his relationship
with his own daughter, have come to the forefront of his work, or to
be more precise they were always there, but with time the picture
seems to have become more honest, less flippant. When Milligan
wrote poems about depression he tried to write 'serious poems', and
as a consequence wrote not-very-good poems. John, by not attempt-
ing to find another voice, another register, by not trying to write
'serious poetry', by simply being honest in the form he's a master of,
writes serious poems that are worth something, that are not dimin-

ished by being surrounded by funny poems or by being funny themselves.

May 2002

> In the doctor's reception the sign read:
> Are you looking after someone over 65
> with mental health problems?
> I read the sign as:
> Are you looking for someone over 65
> with mental health problems?

What Hegley talks about are the things in life that we all share. Family is at the heart of his work and at the heart of our lives: families with us or lost; loved, remembered or feared; the struggle that these relationships can be. It is the big heart that beats so well within the absurd and the surreal, inside the poetry that puts him head and shoulders above other comic poets of his generation; and a writer with heart, love, wit and an alarmingly fresh eye is always something, and someone, to cherish.

A. F. HARROLD is an English poet who has recently taken a turn into children's literature and procrastinatory gardening. He usually divides his time between appearing on stages, pages and in the bath: www.afharrold.com.

Adventures in Achromatopsia

CATHERINE MERRICK

The Island of the Colour-blind was given to me by a friend who was himself red-green colour-blind. This discovery, early in our relationship, illuminated several of his quirks: a terrible dress sense, a preference for Dürer engravings over Impressionist sunsets, a comment made on an early date that our shirts 'matched' (I was in damson, he was in scarlet – the two shades of red clashed horribly). As a biologist, I thought I knew about colour-blindness, but this wonderfully weird book gave me a whole new perspective on the phenomenon.

The author, Dr Oliver Sacks, is an eminent neurologist with an impressive list of bestselling books to his name. The most famous of these is the memorably titled *The Man Who Mistook His Wife for a Hat*, in which I discovered 'visual agnosia' – the complete failure to recognize familiar objects or people – and felt suddenly grateful that my own friend merely mistook his reds and his greens. Dr Sacks has investigated and documented neurological oddities throughout his career, up to and including his own recent loss of one eye to ocular cancer in the acutely personal *The Mind's Eye*. His writing style is scholarly, humane and highly accessible: *The New York Times* has called him 'a kind of poet laureate of contemporary medicine'. Indeed, the medical mystery tour recounted in *The Island of the Colour-blind* (1997) is probably his most poetic offering.

Dr Sacks begins his tale by describing how the visual migraines he

Oliver Sacks, *The Island of the Colour-blind* (1997)
Picador · Pb · 384pp · £9.99 · ISBN 9780330526104

experienced in childhood left him with an abiding interest in colour perception. He also sustained an omnivorous passion for biology in general and for island biogeography in particular: 'Islands have always fascinated me; perhaps they fascinate everyone . . . special places, remote and mysterious, intensely attractive, yet frightening too.' These various interests converged in adulthood when he met two colour-blind patients: one who had lost his colour vision in an accident and another who was born without it. Completely achromatic vision, 'achromatopsia', is seriously disabling, and as rare as red-green colour-blindness is common. So Sacks was intrigued to discover that a tenth of the entire population on the tiny Pacific island of Pingelap was achromatopic. How did these people cope with their condition? How had their culture adapted to accommodate it?

Not content with merely reading up on the subject, Oliver Sacks travelled 7,000 miles to find out, having roped in an American ophthalmologist and an achromatopic physiologist from Norway for a scientific expedition rather akin to those of his Victorian heroes, Darwin and Humboldt.

The answers proved to be complex, reaching beyond neurology to encompass genetics, history and anthropology. Sacks and his colleagues examined the colour-blind people of Pingelap, distributed visual aids and tried to dispel some of the folk myths surrounding *maskun* (Pingelapese for 'not-see'), which included the fear that it progresses to total blindness and the belief that it is caused by mystic curses. In fact, the aetiology is a dramatic genetic bottleneck dating back to 1775, when the atoll's population was slashed to just twenty by a devastating typhoon. Intensive inbreeding saved the community but also brought out the genetic disorder. Tiny, isolated islands like Pingelap, Sacks emphasizes, live very much 'on the edge', both physically and genetically. Typhoons are still a danger and the population still remains at a barely sustainable few hundred. It exists on the edge of stability and the edge of survival.

Pingelap's story of natural disaster and dogged renewal is told without drama, in the author's habitual tone of pragmatic humanism. It is probably no accident that he moves on from Pingelap to describe the abject colonial history of neighbouring Pohnpei, where successive invaders brought infectious diseases, religious crusades and oppressive regimes that decimated the native islanders as effectively as any act of nature. Pohnpei is much larger than Pingelap and it harbours many immigrant communities from nearby atolls. The Pingelapese enclaves on Pohnpei are insular and geographically isolated, something that may have ensured their survival through a troubled recent history, but that also prevented out-breeding. Here, as on their native soil, the Pingelapese show a high rate of *maskun*.

Leaving the island of Pohnpei, *The Island of the Colour-blind* takes a left turn and concludes with a separate episode on the islands of Guam and Rota, linked to the first purely by geography. Dr Sacks defends the book's idiosyncratic structure in his preface:

> I went to Micronesia as a neurologist, or neuroanthropologist, intent on seeing how individuals and communities responded to unusual endemic conditions – a hereditary total colour-blindness on Pingelap and Pohnpei; a progressive, fatal neuro-degenerative disorder on Guam and Rota. But I also found myself riveted by the cultural life and history of these islands . . . If seeing patients, visiting archaeological sites, wandering in rain forests, snorkelling in the reefs, at first seem to bear no relation to each other, they then fused into a single unpartitionable experience, a total immersion in island life.

It is in this spirit that one must read the book: as an idiosyncratic hybrid of travelogue, scientific monograph and detective tale, given coherence and propelled by the author's eclectic interests. He describes the islanders' diet, religion and prevailing attitude towards the disabled with nuanced sympathy. He waxes lyrical about night-fishing and snorkelling, and remarks delightedly on hearing his first cephalopod creation myth on Pohnpei. His sophisticated medical writing often contrasts sharply with a childlike enthusiasm for story-telling. 'The first draft of what I write', Sacks has admitted, 'can be monstrously hyperbolic: I rely on editing.' It can also, it seems, be monstrously erratic, and his editor has wisely collected the footnotes for this book into 65 pages of endnotes. I am seldom tolerant of copi-ous footnotes, finding them distracting and self-indulgent; here, however, they are quite engrossing, being by turns scholarly, personal and just plain bizarre. They certainly disrupt the text, but you may not want to miss them. 'My footnotes are my Prozac,' Sacks once told an interviewer, 'I love writing them.' Since the story itself is a mere 200 pages long, the best approach may be to read it twice: once straight through, and then again complete with all the antidepressant asides.

Throughout *The Island of the Colour-blind*, an odd, yet engaging, authorial personality is apparent. For a man much lauded as a scien-tific communicator, Oliver Sacks is famously shy and socially uneasy – it has been suggested that he has Asperger's syndrome, a suggestion that he himself has met with ambivalence. Certainly, he seems to operate with an unusual directness of mind. Upon hearing that a sea cucumber found off Pingelap may be edible, he immediately sinks his teeth into it ('I found it impossible to get through the leathery integument – it was like trying to eat an old, weathered shoe'). At several points on his journey, he falls into serious physical peril: a near crash-landing in a light aircraft and a violent storm in a tiny boat. Both are recorded with detached curiosity, as indeed is the potentially alarming experience of sampling Pohnpei's local drug, *sakau*. 'I tried to get up, but found I could not . . . "Excellent!" I thought, the neurologist in me aroused. "I have read of this, and now I am experiencing it. Lack of light touch, lack of proprioception – this must be what deafferentation feels like."' This experimental atti-tude to drugs may seem less surprising when it is put in context, for Sacks has admitted to amphetamine addiction as a young man. The habit lasted several years; then one day, while high, he decided to write books instead and quit the amphetamines overnight.

If there is any truth in the Asperger's theory, it clearly does not pre-clude compassion: Dr Sacks has been accused of parading his neuro-logically afflicted patients as a sort of freak show, but although their outlandish conditions may invite this attitude, his interest in them seems at least as humane as it is academic. In *The Man Who Mistook His Wife for a Hat*, he explains, 'I feel myself a naturalist and physician both; and that I am equally interested in diseases and people.' Thus, on the interminable flight from America to Pingelap, he talks to a military nurse, a Christian missionary and a Spam importer, report-ing their contrasting views with journalistic zeal (albeit reserving a certain disapproval for the 'South Seas Spam baron').

When Oliver Sacks visited my local bookshop last year to promote a new book, the queue for autographs stretched right around the building. 'How nice to see this one again,' he commented when I presented him with *The Island of the Colour-blind*. He meant, of course, that it made a change from signing the hundredth copy of *The Mind's Eye*, but his phrasing made me reflect on his recurring theme of sensory perception, and on his own newly diminished power of sight. He could not, in fact, see the book very well with his one remaining eye: the signature was angular and choppy. Then I remembered the words of John Hull, who writes about becoming blind in his memoir *Touching the Rock*: 'when I say I am pleased to see you, what I mean is that I am pleased to meet you, pleased to be with you, glad to be in your presence . . . There is an intimate con-nection between seeing and knowing.' Indeed there is, and it is in this wider sense that Dr Sacks allows his readers to glimpse the Island of the Colour-blind for themselves.

CATHERINE MERRICK is a malaria biologist and university lecturer. She is very grateful for the standard-issue genes that allow her to see in glorious technicolor.

Flashman's Nemesis

BRIAN PAYNE

In *Slightly Foxed* No.33, Andrew Nixon paid homage to George MacDonald Fraser's splendid creation, the appalling Flashman; and Patrick Mercer, himself an infantryman, drew attention to *Quartered Safe Out Here*, Fraser's autobiographical account of his own service as an Other Rank in the Border Regiment. But both omitted mention of Fraser's other marvellous creation, the infamous Private McAuslan, the dirtiest soldier ever to grace the tartan of a Highland regiment.

McAuslan, whose adventures are described in three books – *The General Danced at Dawn* (1970), *McAuslan in the Rough* (1974) and *The Sheikh and the Dustbin* (1988) – is an invention whose time has now passed. He is, in the words of any regular soldier, 'A Thing'. Always offending the tender susceptibilities of the professional soldiers among whom he is deposited, Private McAuslan, a shrunken, grey, greasy and shambling figure, is the very antithesis of the elegant Flashman. The premise is simple – whatever is good and noble about soldiering is subverted by the shameful conduct of McAuslan, who never intentionally behaves badly, but who is such an excuse for a soldier that disaster trails him.

His time has passed because the books were written in a period when many readers had an extensive memory of serving in one of the armed services, either during the Second World War or as part of

George MacDonald Fraser's Private McAuslan books – *The General Danced at Dawn* (1970), *McAuslan in the Rough* (1974) and *The Sheikh and the Dustbin* (1988) – are now available in a single volume: *The Complete McAuslan* · HarperCollins · Pb · 608pp · £10.99 · ISBN 9780006513711.

National Service. They – we – all knew about similar 'Things'. We had encountered them throughout our service, however short. The perspiring figure pan-bashing in the cookhouse, the perpetual adornment of the guardroom cells, the one man who could be relied upon to leave his weapon behind or drop a shell on his foot – they are familiar. I had one called Gunner . . . but I won't name him, for that would be cruel. The brilliance of McAuslan was that George MacDonald Fraser could use him as a vehicle to tell the story of soldiering in a way that rang true to those who had experienced it. His McAuslan books were funny in much the same way as *The Navy Lark* was on the wireless – full of little jokes and subtleties that the reader recognized from his or her own experience.

The stories are told by Dand McNeill, a platoon commander and long-suffering owner and guardian of Private McAuslan. They refer to an unspecified Highland regiment in that period immediately after the last war when infantry battalions were garrisoned around the world keeping the peace. In these stories, the parent unit starts in North Africa and is brought home to Scotland. McAuslan remains a constant theme, but other characters are drawn in, and they populate the familiar family of a good regiment going about peacetime duties. The Pipe Major and his early-morning sonic attacks on the junior officers, the awful moment when McAuslan stands on his glory and demands a court martial, the perfection of the description of an inter-regimental golf match – all are tales to treasure.

Dand McNeill was Fraser himself, the battalion that of the Gordon Highlanders. In creating McAuslan, Fraser brought together a description of all the 'Things' that he had served with as an Other Rank and had commanded as a subaltern when he was commissioned. None of the tales could be attributed to one individual – Fraser was too canny for that – but each was instantly recognizable as being plausible. So many of us had experienced something similar, an impending disaster that would outrage our superiors, that would call down shame and punishment on us and, more importantly, besmirch the good name of the regiment, ship or squadron. Often unfathom-able to civilians, the stories were for those who had served, a series of private jokes.

I had a long and happy discussion with the author about McAuslan. The Border Regiment had been part of the 17th (Indian) Division in Burma – called the Black Cats because of their divisional identification flash. My father was there at the same time, com-manding a platoon and later a company in the Royal Scots. He had fought in the same sort of intense battles as Fraser, but elsewhere. He had enjoyed *Quartered Safe Out Here*, thinking it as good an account as any, and I had caught him with a far-away expression, the book on his lap, when he had borrowed my copy of the McAuslan anthology. He had died by the time I could waylay Fraser, which I did quite shamelessly at the Oxford Literary Festival.

I told him about my father's enjoyment of his books. He in return told me an awful story about my father's regiment, and confirmed that the battalion called 'The Royals' in the McAuslan tale about the golf competition was, as my father recalled, the very same Royal Scots. Flashman was not mentioned once.

Short in stature, and modest, George MacDonald Fraser made a lasting impression on me. The rumbustious nature of the Flashman novels had suggested he would be a polished raconteur, while the affectionate way in which McAuslan is depicted had presented a more tolerant man, wise before his time in the ways of the fighting soldier. I found the understanding, protective and long-suffering Dand McNeill to be the true nature of the author. So I commend McAuslan to you, even if you don't quite appreciate the fine detail of the jokes. The stories are of a time now gone, for the McAuslans of this age do not survive the selection process of the modern armed services. But, above all, I commend George MacDonald Fraser to you. Read all his books, and there you will find your man.

BRIAN PAYNE, once a regular soldier, is a barrister and might, if he is very lucky, have his first novel published shortly.

Hurricane Clarice

MICHAEL MARETT-CROSBY

The sleeper lounge is old-fashioned British Rail, all tartan carpet, smeared tables and microwave cuisine. Tonight it contains a gathering of solitaries, all of us making separate journeys to London. The man beside me is still working, though it's nearly ten o'clock.

By chance we order the same whisky. We raise our plastic glasses, embarrassed in a very British way. I want to encourage him. He is at war with a pile of papers. But he is wishing me good luck as well. He has been glancing at the author's face on the back cover of my novel. She does rather stare.

Her name is Clarice Lispector, one of the most original and fascinating writers of the twentieth century. She is the author of nine novels and several collections of short stories, all written in Portuguese. She was born in 1920, not as Clarice but as Chaya, the daughter of Ukrainian Jewish parents. From this beginning she was to become, improbably, the doyenne of Brazilian literature.

Ukraine to Brazil – who makes that journey? In 1921, young

The following novels by Clarice Lispector are available in an English translation: *Near to the Wild Heart* (1943) · New Directions · Pb · 220pp · $15.95 · ISBN 9780811220026; *Apples in the Dark* (1961) · Haus · Hb · 446pp · £12.99 · ISBN 9781906598457; *The Passion According to G.H.* (1964) · University of Minnesota · Pb · 194pp · $15.95 · ISBN 9780811219686; *The Stream of Life* (1973) · University of Minnesota · Pb · 148pp · £14 · ISBN 9780816617821; and *The Hour of the Star* (1977) · New Directions · Pb · 128pp · $12.95 · ISBN 9780811219495. Benjamin Moser's wonderful biography of her is also in print: *Why This World* (2009) · Haus · Hb · 544pp · £20 · ISBN 9781906598426.

Chaya did, her family fleeing the pogroms that erupted in the region after the First World War. Brazil took them in. Once there, the family adapted their first names to their new home. Thus Chaya became Clarice. 'I am a Brazilian,' she wrote, 'and that is that.'

Despite her confidence, she didn't immediately fit in. 'People here look at me as if I come straight from the zoo,' she wrote in 1941, to which she added, 'I entirely agree.' From the back of my book, she stares with wide eyes from a pale face, 'that rare person', it has been said, 'who looked like Marlene Dietrich and wrote like Virginia Woolf'. Indeed her writing style proved to be as alluring as her appearance. The refugees' daughter was to create a new national literature.

She was a clever, even impish child, though her youth was overshadowed by her mother's paralysis. Little Clarice wrote magical stories, wanting to heal her. They did not work, and her mother died when Clarice was 10. But still, just three years later, Clarice wrote that she knew she would have to be a writer, although she later toyed with the idea of becoming a prison lawyer.

In 1943 she married Maury Gurgel Valente, an unlikely choice not least because Maury was Catholic. He was also a diplomat, and so the 23-year-old Clarice embarked on a life of travel and cocktail parties. She would move with him from post to post, variously Naples, Berne, even Torquay. She did not much care for Switzerland, calling it 'a cemetery of sensations', and she found Torquay boring, but she did like England: 'The lack of sun. The lack of beauty. It all moves me.'

This emphasis on absence – the lack of sun and lack of beauty – finds its way into Clarice's books. A sense of place and a straightforward plot are often missing, but the woman who once dreamt of reforming prisons writes with rare beauty of confined women breaking free, and nowhere with more power than in her first novel, *Near to the Wild Heart*, published in 1943, the year in which she married.

It caused a storm; indeed one critic wrote of 'Hurricane Clarice'. Everyone wanted to know who this woman was who wrote so differently from anything that had been known in Brazil before.

'In search of the thing itself':
Clarice Lispector

Near to the Wild Heart takes its title from James Joyce's *Portrait of the Artist as a Young Man*, part of a passage where Joyce describes his hero Stephen Dedalus's freedom. 'Where was his boyhood now?' Joyce writes. 'He was alone. He was unheeded, happy and near to the wild heart of life.'

Near to the Wild Heart opens with Joana, a little girl much like Clarice had been, intent on knowing everything. She hears her father's typewriter and notices the silences in between the clacking of the keys. She looks out of the window at 'the great world of the chickens-that-did-not-know-they-were-about-to-die'. (Clarice remained worried about chickens throughout her writing life and 'The Hen' is among the best of her short stories.) Joana wants to catch the moment and the next moment and the meaning of it all. Her father wonders, what will become of her?

The chapters on Joana's childhood are interlaced with Joana as an older woman, married by this time to a man called Otávio. He is suitable, and boring. The child of freedom has become an adult caught behind the bars of respectability, and it is tempting here to find autobiographical parallels. Did Clarice see that her own marriage to Maury would end unhappily? It feels as if Clarice explores not only her own future through Joana, but something much larger. 'Adults are sad and solitary,' Clarice said in her last broadcast. 'Children have their imagination. They are free.'

Clarice's characters, especially her women, are searching for freedom. Plot and place slip away; she is an author intent upon the story of the mind. As we come to know Joana in *Near to the Wild Heart*, the comparisons between her youth and married years grow painful. Joana's life shrinks until she is absolutely stuck.

Perhaps this is what happened to Clarice herself. After fifteen years of diplomatic life she separated from Maury and returned to Rio with her two children. Then her son Pedro was diagnosed with schizophrenia. For a time, she scraped a living writing make-up tips. An editor described Clarice in the late 1950s as bringing 'an anguished silence' with her into his office. No one was reading her books. She was as stuck as her first heroine had been.

In the second half of *Near to the Wild Heart*, it turns out that Joana's husband Otávio is not quite as respectable as he had seemed. He has a lover called Lídia and she is everything that Joana is not. 'Why is she so powerful?' Joana asks. 'I can't imagine that because I haven't spent my afternoons sewing, this makes me inferior to her. Or does it? It does, it doesn't, it does, it doesn't.' Eventually, Joana tells Lídia to keep Otávio. Why? A bitter reason: 'I do not bring peace to anyone.'

Thereafter Joana enters a space deep inside herself, moving from the ordinary world into what Clarice describes as 'a fluid region, quiescent and unfathomable'. It is in this inner life that her heroines often find meaning, not a retreat into childhood but an advance into experiencing the world anew.

Take Ana for example. She is the heroine of Clarice's fine short story 'Love'. Ana, like Joana and like Clarice herself, has a house and children and a safe, ordinary life, or, as Clarice puts it, 'She had gradually emerged to discover that life could be lived without happiness.' In place of joy, Ana is needed, with things to do. She manages for all but one hour in each day. In this space she rides the trams, going nowhere.

On one such trip, she sees a blind man. 'Like some strange music, the world started up again.' What world? The world as Clarice Lispector wants us to see it – nightmarish and lawless, but exciting for being crammed with secrets. 'The world was so rich that it was rotting,' she writes. 'The very crust of the days she had forged had broken.'

This is not just about seeing pretty things. Ana feels deep nausea when she experiences as if for the first time the hunger of the poor. 'The murder was deep.' The wild heart of life contains beauty and also pain. This is what I love in Clarice Lispector's writing, this wild heart. Hers are novels about seeing the extraordinary in the ordinary. She is a tutor of the strangeness and the wonder of things.

In terms of plot, I cannot tell you much more. Clarice is not bothered with this-then-that. 'To see her as a novelist is like calling Plato a playwright,' Lorrie Moore has written of Lispector's work.

In time, Clarice met with success and adulation. She is still held in high regard in Brazil and among academics. There is a lot written about her, much of it very complicated. She can be perplexing and is a nightmare to translate. But Clarice Lispector is a writer who keeps life alive. She just does not believe that anyone has limits.

It is morning. The sleeper feels like an intruder, moving jarringly through north London, giving way to commuter trains. My friend with the whisky is back at his papers, now armed with coffee. I have spent the night with a strange and wonderful woman. 'If I had to give a title to my life,' Clarice once wrote, 'it would be this: I am in search of the thing itself.' She is a chronicler of freedom like no other writer I know.

MICHAEL MARETT-CROSBY writes when he is not reading. His first novel, *Two Thirds Man*, is doing the rounds of agents. He stays optimistic amidst their silence by working on a sequel.

The Man in the Lavender Suit

DEREK PARKER

I've always thought journals and letters among the best of bedside books. The entries, for one thing, are just long enough, usually, to end as drowsiness begins to be irresistible. I first came across one of Horace Walpole's letters in an anthology, and thought it was as entertaining as one of Byron's. I looked out more of them; they too were as entertaining as Byron's – maybe even more so. I had recently given up buying, volume by volume as they came out, the great Murray edition of Byron's letters, on the grounds that they had become too expensive; a decision I now regret with inexpressible bitterness. But maybe there was an affordable collected edition of Walpole's.

There was indeed. It was published by Yale and edited by W. S. Lewis, who had worked on the project for 46 years, and published the final 48th volume in 1983. I don't know whether it's now possible to find a complete set; if one could, it would I guess be astronomically expensive. I gave up the idea. But fortunately single volumes pop up here and there on the Internet, as indeed do excellent selections – my own favourite, by my own bedside, came from a bookshop found on iLibris, published in 1930 and a good-looking book as well as a good anthology.

Most people, if they think of Walpole at all, remember him as the author of the Gothic horror story *The Castle of Otranto* – popular enough in its time, still readable and sometimes read. He's also

You can read all of Walpole's letters, free, on your computer: go to
http://www.library.yale.edu/walpole/collections/digital_collection_corr.html

remembered for Strawberry Hill, the most famous house in Georgian England (open to the public now as it was in his own time, when he even set up an advance booking system). His *Essay on Modern Gardening* has its virtues. But the best of his life went into his letters. Sir Walter Scott called him 'the best letter-writer in the English language'; Byron thought his letters 'incomparable' – and he knew something about writing a good letter.

The son of Sir Robert Walpole, Prime Minister under the first two Georges, Walpole was provided by his father with a large income skimmed from the public purse, and was thus free to devote his time to whatever activity appealed to him – playing with Patapan or Tonton, his dogs, planning and executing the creation of his toy castle, writing his gothic romance and a few other books. He was a Whig MP for 27 years – for Callington, in Cornwall, which he never visited, then for Castle Rising, in Norfolk, and finally for King's Lynn. He took politics seriously, without actually taking a serious active role in them. Setting down social gossip and scandal in fifty years of letters to a huge variety of friends was his main occupation and pleasure.

Horace Walpole in the library of Strawberry Hill, by J. H. Müntz

A little man in a lavender suit, with ruffles and lace-frilled shirt, silver-embroidered white silk waistcoat, silk stockings and gold-buckled shoes, he found his way into every fashionable salon and knew everyone who was worth knowing: from members of the royal family and the government to the most beautiful and notorious women of the age – La Belle Jennings, Arabella Churchill, the Duchess of Kendal and Mrs Fitzherbert. He seems not to have been inordinately attractive: his voice was rough and his laugh forced and coarse, and for the second half of his life he was crippled with gout. His manners were formal but less than considerate – one of his dogs always joined him at table, sometimes accompanied by a pet squirrel.

He adored dogs – a guest in a somewhat dull house, he was pleased that at least 'there were two or three children, and two or three-and-forty dogs; I generally prefer both to what common people call Christians'. He was appalled at the general view of dogs, complaining in 1760 that

> in London the streets are a very picture of the murder of the innocents – one drives over nothing but poor dead dogs! The dear, good-natured, honest, sensible creatures! Christ! How can anybody hurt them? Nobody could but those Cherokees the English, who desire no better than to be halloo'd to blood – one day, Admiral Byng, the next Lord George Sackville, and today the poor dogs!

Walpole attended most of the great royal occasions of his lifetime (as a boy he had kissed the hand of King George I and he lived to see the accession of George III). In November 1760 he sent one of his correspondents a long and vivid account of the funeral of George II, 'the yeomen of the guard crying out for help, oppressed by the immense weight of the coffin'. Amid the solemnity appeared the Duke of Newcastle:

> He fell into a fit of crying the moment he came into the chapel, and flung himself back in a stall, the Archbishop hovering over him with a smelling-bottle; but in two minutes his curiosity got the better of his hypocrisy, and he ran about the chapel with his glass to spy who was or was not there, spying with one hand, and mopping his eyes with the other. Then returned the fear of catching cold, and the Duke of Cumberland, who was sinking with heat, felt himself weighed down, and turning round, found it was the Duke of Newcastle standing on his train, to avoid the chill of the marble.

Such eccentricities delighted him – he was especially fond of the account of a small pew in Gloucester cathedral, 'hung with green damask, with curtains of the same; a small corner cupboard, painted, carved, and gilt, for books in one corner, and two troughs of a bird-cage, with seeds and water . . . It belongs to a Mrs Cotton, who, having lost a favourite daughter, is convinced her soul is transmigrated into a robin-redbreast. The chapter indulge this whim, as she contributes abundantly to glaze, whitewash and ornament the church.'

Royal and noble amours always entertained him. He watched with interest the progress of George II's admiration for Elizabeth Chudleigh, who appeared at a Ranelagh masquerade as Iphigenia, 'but so naked that you would have taken her for Andromeda' – that was on the famous occasion when the witty Lady Mary Wortley Montagu remarked that Miss Chudleigh 'was Iphigenia for the sacrifice, but so naked the high priest might easily inspect the entrails of the victim'. Walpole looked on as the king presented her with a 35-guinea watch, and later kissed her in public. She became the royal mistress, despite the protests of Augustus Hervey and the Duke of Kingston, concurrently her husbands.

Walpole never married, and it seems likely he was either homosexual or asexual – which did not prevent him from admiring a handsome woman. Marie Antoinette seems to have been his ideal: she 'shot through the room like an aerial being, all brightness and grace and without seeming to touch earth . . . Hebes and Floras, and Helens and Graces, are street-walkers to her. She is a statue of beauty, when standing or sitting; grace itself when she moves . . . For beauty [at Versailles] I saw none, for the Queen effaced all the rest.' He also much admired the Duchess of Richmond, 'fair and blooming as when she was a bride' despite the fact that she 'takes care that the house of Richmond shall not be extinguised: she again lies in, after having been with child seven-and-twenty times'.

No one enjoyed a party more than Walpole, but he did become

Horace Walpole by
Sir Thomas Lawrence

irritated if they went on too long: 'Silly dissipation increases, and without an object', he told Sir Horace Mann in 1777 – an American fashion, he fancied. 'The present folly is late hours. Everybody tries to be particular by being too late. It is the fashion now to go to Ranelagh two hours after it is over. You may not believe this, but it is literal. The music ends at ten; the company go at twelve. Lord Derby's cook lately gave him warning. The man owned he liked his place, but said he should be killed by dressing suppers at three in the morning.' When he, Walpole, tried to engage a housemaid and asked why she wanted to leave her present place, she told him she 'could not support the hours she kept; that her lady never went to bed till three or four in the morning. "Bless me, child," I said, "why, you tell me you live with a bishop's wife: I never heard that Mrs North gamed or raked so late." "No, sir," said she, "but she takes three hours undressing."'

He never indulged in the great vice of the age, gambling, but happily reported its extremities: at White's club, in 1750, 'a man dropped down dead at the door, was carried in; the club immediately made bets whether he was dead or not, and when they were going to bleed him, the wagerers for his death interposed, and said it would affect the fairness of the bet'. Twenty-five years later, a young man 'betted £1,500 that a man could live twelve hours under water; hired a desperate fellow, sunk him in a ship, by way of experiment, and both ship and man have not appeared since'.

If he had a vice, if it *is* a vice, it was his love of fires, 'the only horrid sight that is fine'. His servant was ordered to wake him at any news of a conflagration. In February 1755 (he told his friend Richard Bentley) he was awakened in the middle of the night, threw on his slippers and the fine embroidered suit he had taken off that evening, and dashed off toward St James's.

I ran to Bury Street, and stepped into a pipe that was broken up for water. It would have made a picture – the horror of the flames, the snow, the day breaking with difficulty through so foul a night, and my figure, all mud and gold. It put me in mind of Lady Margaret Herbert's providence, who asked somebody for a pretty pattern for a nightcap. 'Lord!' said they, 'what signifies the pattern of a nightcap?' – 'Oh! Child,' said she, 'but, you know, in case of fire.' Two young beauties were conveyed out of a window in their shifts. There have been two more great fires. Alderman Belchier's house at Epsom, that belonged to the Prince [of Wales], is burnt, and Beckford's fine house in the country, with pictures and furniture of a great value. He says, 'Oh! I have an odd fifty thousand pounds in a drawer: I will build it up again: it won't be above a thousand pounds a-piece difference to my thirty children.'

Like most men, Walpole grumbled at change – manners were becoming terse and coarse: 'all paraphrases and expletives are so much in disuse, that I suppose soon the only way of making love will be to say "Lie down."' He took his old age gracefully, however, to the point when he was 'an unfinished skeleton of seventy-seven, on whose bones the worms have left just so much skin as prevents my being nailed up yet'. He died in 1797 and, as the essayist Austin Dobson put it, 'for diversity of interest and perpetual entertainment, for the constant surprises of an unique species of wit, for happy and unexpected turns of phrase, for graphic characterisation and clever anecdote, for playfulness, pungency, irony, persiflage, there is nothing in English like his correspondence.'

DEREK PARKER lives in Sydney with his wife Julia; they have edited twelve anthologies of poems particularly suitable for each of the twelve signs of the Zodiac, just published in book form and as e-books.

Of Bembo, Caslon and Clairvaux

ROGER HUDSON

The Folio Society was founded 65 years ago and has been gradually undergoing apotheosis into a National Treasure, to join Radio 4, the Proms, Alan Bennett and the London taxi. Like some hound of heaven, it is in unrelenting pursuit of quality, its books by the best authors old and new produced using the best methods old and new, and new illustrators too, striving to end up with the best that mind, hand and eye can do.

It is not surprising that members of Folio and subscribers to *Slightly Foxed* are quite often one and the same. Those for whom reading is an important part of life may well hanker after something more in the way of the book beautiful than an airport bookstall or the stickered stacks of three-for-two can offer. Not always, you understand: the motives of someone who only has Folio books on view might be suspect. Have they been bought as a short cut to cultivation, for display only? But for inveterate spine scanners who convince themselves that books are an indicator of character, it is always reassuring to

Joan Hassall
Pride and Prejudice

spot some Folio titles mixed in on a person's shelves, to know he or she has succumbed to their tactile and visual pleasures – the beautifully engineered slipcases, the proper cloth or buckram bindings, the paper that remains unfaded, the well-chosen typefaces, the attention to proportion and space. There is anticipatory pleasure reading the litany of specifications in each year's catalogue: 'Quarter-bound cloth with Modigliani paper sides', 'Bound in blocked buckram', 'Set in Bembo, in Adobe Caslon, in Palatino', even 'in Elysium with Clairvaux display'. It is like going to bed with an Elizabeth David cook book after dining off baked beans (four-volume boxed set, yours for £19.95 from Folio, as an introductory offer).

And then there are the pictures, and the designs on the bindings. Some people are snooty about illustrating grown-up fiction, vapouring on about how their imaginations will generate all the images they need. The riposte to that is Dickens and Phiz, Surtees and Leech, Sherlock Holmes and Sidney Paget. In the past Folio has added to this roll of honour with such achievements as Joan Hassall's wood engravings for Jane Austen, Simon Brett's for a gamut running from Keats and Shelley to *Legends of the Grail*, Charles Keeping's drawings for the 16-volume Dickens, Edward Bawden's linocuts for Malory's *Morte d'Arthur*. Folio threw a lifeline to illustrators as work for advertisers and magazines began to dry up from the 1950s, and it continues to be the one firm regularly commissioning pictures for something other than children's books. The chances it offers young artists who have managed to survive the near-death in art schools of academic drawing and the bias towards the non-representational, if not the downright conceptual, are beyond price.

Current and recent Folio lists are testimony to how these chances have been seized. Take for example Anna Bhushan's drawings for *The Bhagavad Gita*, Michael Kirkham's for *Of Human Bondage* or Matthew Richardson's collage images for Albert Camus' *The Outsider*. The latter was the winner of the inaugural Book Illustration Competition run jointly by Folio and the House of Illustration and has now won one of the 2012 V&A Illustration Awards for its cover. Any idea that Folio is wedded to the representational or conventional – except of course for non-fiction and history, where period pictures and photographs are the norm – will quickly be dispelled by a look at the current catalogue or website. There too the bindings for Clausewitz's *On War* and for G. E. R. Lloyd's *Greek Science* show what can be done

Simon Brett
Legends of the Grail

with pattern and symbol to capture the overall theme of a book.

There is something of the Apostolic Succession, of passing on the sacred flame, about the origins of the Folio Society. The Golden Cockerel Press had been perhaps the most distinguished of the inter-war private presses, and Christopher Sandford, one of the three founders of Folio, owned it in 1947. Not only that, but Folio began life sharing the Golden Cockerel offices in Soho. And it has recently reissued *The Four Gospels*, *The Canterbury Tales* and Chaucer's *Troilus and Criseyde* in facsimile which, with their Eric Gill illustrations, many consider to be the Golden Cockerel at its best. The other Folio founders were Alan Bott, who had already created the Book Society and the paperback imprint Pan Books, so could bring book trade expertise, and Charles Ede whose idea it was. Ede claimed he could only bring enthusiasm, though in fact he ran the show, giving the firm much of its ethos and flavour. They had to cope with paper rationing but post-war there were many who felt starved of quality and were longing for anything that tried to raise standards above the 'utility' norm. In retrospect Folio can be seen as part of a high-minded Welfare-Stateism signalled by the founding of the Arts Council and the BBC Third Programme and culminating in the 1951 Festival of Britain.

To begin with the books were sold via bookshops, but this did not work and it was only when members started to be recruited directly through press advertising in 1949–50, and were offered an incentive in the form of a free 'presentation volume', that things started to look up. The deal was much the same as today: you were asked to commit to taking four books a year. Early titles had jackets but the first slipcase came in 1954; almost from the start introductions were specially commissioned for virtually all books.

The Society could not afford to gamble so stuck almost entirely to classic fiction and poetry, but gradually history and ancient history, travel and biography, humour, children's books and modern fiction were added to the mix, and boxed sets were produced as well as individual volumes. Conventional publishers have always envied Folio for being able to sound out its membership about what future choices it favoured; what's more, it could then establish a reasonably accurate number to print by getting advance orders once the yearly catalogue had been mailed out. They also used to assume that it could afford better production standards because it paid so little in royalties, since most of its books were old enough to be out of copyright. With more and more twentieth-century authors and recent translations of foreign-language titles, this has long ceased to be the case.

Charles Ede said he only wanted to work in a business where he could do everything himself, so in 1971 he gave up Folio and instead became a leading dealer in classical antiquities. One of the most noticeable trends over the next two decades was the move into history, which for years has been the Society's biggest-selling category. This produced a number of books in which Folio's editorial input

was greatly increased: selecting material from different sources, ordering it, writing linking passages. A prime example was Macaulay's *History of England*, where his original volumes covering 1685 to 1702 were extended backwards and forwards in time by Peter Rowland, using Macaulay's essays and articles.

Here I must declare a bias, because I compiled quite a number of such books for the Society, making a selection for the series called 'Eighteenth-century Memoirs' from the original four volumes of William Hickey's, which was illustrated by the wonderful John Lawrence and bound using Ann Muir's

Michael Kirkham
Of Human Bondage

78

marbled paper; then selections from the journalism of the great war reporter William Howard Russell and from the copious literature of the British in India, for the 'Epics of Empire and Exploration' series, with brilliant pastiche Victorian blocked bindings by David Eccles. I was also let loose on Queen Victoria's Jubilee years, the English Civil War through women's eyes and the Grand Tour.

What might be termed the Gavron effect started kicking in at the end of the 1980s. Bob Gavron, creator of the St Ives printing group, had bought Folio in 1982, and he was responsible for its major expansion. There were years when membership was well over 100,000 and the number of new editions over 80 (in 1987 the figures had been 36,000 and 25). The task of maintaining production standards under this pressure while absorbing the impact and possibilities of computerization and constantly refreshing the reservoir of artists fell to Joe Whitlock Blundell, who had arrived in 1986.

As well as overseeing such enterprises as the 47-volume complete Trollope, the facsimiles of great late Victorian or Edwardian children's books illustrated by the likes of the Detmold brothers and Arthur Rackham, and Andrew Lang's Rainbow Fairy Books, Joe has also been behind the remarkable series of limited editions which have added another dimension to Folio: the William Blake *Night Thoughts*, with *Gray's Poems* to come, reproducing his illustrations never published in his lifetime and subsequently scattered round the world's museums, just as was done in Folio's earlier Blake *Inferno* and *Paradise Lost*; the ongoing Letterpress Shakespeare and the King James Version of the Bible, both uncluttered and eminently readable; medieval facsimiles such as the Hereford *Mappa Mundi*, its colouring restored, the *Fitzwilliam Book of Hours*, *The Luttrell Psalter*

Anna Bhushan
The Bhagavad Gita

and a poignant modern one, *The South Polar Times* by the men of Scott's two expeditions, published on the centenary of his death last year.

With its membership somewhere a little below 100,000 now, about equally divided between Britain and North America, and the number of new editions around 60 a year plus some limited editions, the Folio Society must be well placed to benefit from the advent of the e-book. It can become one of the best comforts and recourses, not merely for those in (one hopes, irrational) dread of some book-less dystopia, along the lines of that in *Fahrenheit 451* (Folio edition, December 2011), but also for the many who have become accustomed to the screen but want a regular treat, a reminder of the best of what reading can be.

ROGER HUDSON compiled, selected or edited over a dozen books for Folio while also working for a number of other publishers, including his old firm, John Murray.

The Folio Society is at 44 Eagle Street, London WCIR 4FS, telephone 020 7400 4200. Its website is at www.foliosociety.com. The illustrations in this article have been substantially reduced in size from the originals.

Talking to the Major

DENNIS BUTTS

Percy F. Westerman (1876–1959) was one of the most popular writers of boys' adventure stories from the 1920s to the 1950s. In their brightly coloured dust-jackets his historical tales – books about the Great War or the early days of aviation – sold in their thousands, and in the Thirties he was acclaimed as *the* most popular boys' author in a referendum run by the *Daily Sketch*. By the time he died he had written nearly 200 books, which had been translated into many languages, and achieved sales of one and a half million copies. Many readers of *Slightly Foxed* will remember the excitement they felt when they first encountered the exploits of Standish, the flying detective, in such tales as *The Amir's Ruby* (1932) or *Standish Gets His Man* (1938).

THRILLING YARNS

B. Lodge

Yet when, in the 1960s, having written a little book about Robert Louis Stevenson, I became increasingly interested in the evolution of the adventure story, one name kept coming up that no one seemed to know anything about – that of Percy F. Westerman. So I decided to investigate. I sent off shoals of letters – to publishers, to libraries, to illustrators and to his old school – but without much success. Terence Cuneo, one of Westerman's most distinguished illustrators, for example, wrote me a charming reply, saying how much he had always enjoyed illustrating Westerman's stories but that he had never actually

All of Percy F. Westerman's novels are out of print.

met the author. The publisher would send him a book, he would decide what scenes he wanted to depict, and he'd simply get on with it. A retired master from Portsmouth Grammar School, Westerman's *alma mater*, reported: 'I have consulted the *Portmuthian* [the school magazine] for the years Percy Westerman could have been at the school, but the search was in vain: he does not seem to have done anything spectacular enough to get his name in the magazine.' I was getting nowhere.

I finally struck lucky in 1967 when, in response to a letter sent to Westerman's widow at an address supplied by his main publisher, Blackie, I was contacted by Westerman's son, Major J. F. C. Westerman. After apologizing for his (near-faultless) typing, he wrote me a long and detailed letter about his father, and invited me to visit him at his home in Dorset.

Recently widowed, he lived on his own in a classically picturesque thatched cottage, with a stream running by, in the village of Winterborne Zelstone. He would have been in his late sixties when I first met him, and hale and hearty in manner and appearance. When I wrote later, saying that I hoped my visit had not tired him, he replied: 'Although nearer 70 than 60, I can assure you that I feel far from getting on . . . and I feel that my yachting keeps me fit, active and relatively "tough".'

Major Westerman was a delightful person and, blessed with a sympathetic manner and a good memory, also a gifted raconteur. Although my main interest at that time was in his father, Major Westerman told me quite a lot about himself. He was an only child, and after leaving school had served at various times in the army, the newly established Royal Flying Corps and the Royal Navy. He had travelled all over the world in the services, and had also written quite a few boys' adventure stories in the style of his father.

He told me his father had failed in his ambition to join the Royal Navy because of poor eyesight, and so, after leaving school, he had obtained a post as a clerk in the dockyards. Then, in order to supplement his salary, he had begun writing magazine articles about his two great hobbies, cycling and sailing. He wrote his first full-length book as the result of a bet. At the age of 8, J. F. C. Westerman – 'Jack', as he was always known in the family – had chickenpox, and his father, Percy, was reading him a boys' book of the time. Eventually Percy said, 'What tosh!' His wife overheard him and bet him sixpence that he couldn't do better. So Westerman, who was by now an experienced journalist but not yet a novelist, sat down and wrote *A Lad of Grit*, which was published by Blackie in 1909. This story about the adventures on land and sea in Restoration days of young Aubrey Wentworth, including his exploits in the West Indies among Algerian pirates, did well, and from then on he never looked back.

Sometimes, his son told me, Westerman wrote three or four books a year, varying them between historical novels in the tradition of Walter Scott and G. A. Henty, and modern, more realistic stories about wars and criminal activities, usually involving aeroplanes or ships. All his life he enjoyed sailing, although, apart from one trip to the Channel Islands, he never actually went abroad. His descriptions of foreign lands were always based upon research, and he believed in good grammar and historical accuracy. He was 'a stickler for the things that are right'.

According to Jack, his father was a strict disciplinarian but with a sympathetic manner. During the Second World War he became a member of the local Home Guard, and when his son, now a lieutenant in the army, arrived home on leave, Percy always insisted on saluting him. He was methodical and worked to a strict regime, writing in longhand and using a relief nib and an ink-bottle, never a fountain pen. He generally wrote after his evening meal from 6 p.m. till 3 in the morning. He never worked from a synopsis but wrote at great speed in a beautiful copperplate hand, and the manuscripts were typed up by a professional typist. Usually a book took him six weeks to write, and then he knocked off for a fortnight before starting a new one.

Although Jack himself published no fewer than thirty books between 1929 and 1953 – adventure stories, such as *The Ocean Bandits* (1934), which are very like his father's, so that collectors are often confused – he told me very little about them. My impression was that he didn't take them very seriously. There were very few of either his or his father's books in the cottage.

Major Westerman and I met and corresponded several times during the spring and summer of 1968, and he was always welcoming and generous. Despite his age, he had recently bought a converted motor-torpedo boat, and was planning to sail away to the Mediterranean. 'I want to see the Greek islands again before I die,' he told me. So he was clearing his cottage and insisted on presenting me with numerous souvenirs of his father. I protested that they were probably of financial as well as literary value. 'I can't be bothered, old boy,' he said. 'If you don't take them, they're going in the dustbin.' I'm sure he meant what he said. So he piled on me the typescripts of some of his father's unpublished novels, his scrapbooks, and various other miscellaneous items such as his parents' ration books from the Second World War. These I have subsequently lodged in the Library at the University of Worcester.

Looking back now, one can see that Percy F. Westerman was a figure of his times, an interesting but not a great writer. None of his books are still in print, although they can often be found second-hand. They are still worth looking at for the (sometimes accidentally amusing) light they throw on our ideas of air and sea technology in the early twentieth century, such as *Winning His Wings* (1918), a very readable account of how a young cadet learns to fly at a training school and eventually graduates to wartime combat in France.

The historical novels, such as *The Young Cavalier* (1911), will find readers, too, among those who still admire the works of Henty. But it is perhaps the stories of the First World War, such as *The Dispatch-Riders* (1915) and *To the Fore with the Tanks!* (1918), with their very revealing contemporary attitudes towards battle, courage and patriotism, which may prove to be of more enduring historical interest. Westerman's story-telling, too, despite its obvious limitations, has its own kind of competence and professional integrity, which is not to be despised.

I wish now that I had spent more time talking to the Major about his own remarkable career. After our last meeting in the summer of 1968 we stayed in touch for a few more months, but then I heard no more; and when I returned to Winterborne Zelstone the following year, he had gone. New owners had moved into his cottage. They knew about the Major. 'Yes, he reached the Mediterranean,' they said – he had sent a postcard to their neighbours. But they had heard nothing since.

More recent research has revealed that he sailed the Mediterranean very happily for several years, until his boat sank in a severe gale in Gibraltar Harbour in 1982, after which he moved to the Costa del Sol, where he died in 1991 at the age of 90. What a man!

After National Service in the RAF, DENNIS BUTTS read English at St Catherine's Society, Oxford, after which he taught in various parts of the country for many years. His most recent book, *Children's Literature and Social Change*, was published in 2010.

Wells of Memory

CHRISTIAN TYLER

I don't remember who gave me the fat red book of short stories by
H. G. Wells. But I do remember reading it compulsively as a
teenager, with frissons of fear as well as pleasure. Wells was a favourite
in those days, alongside Somerset Maugham, Conan Doyle and de
Maupassant. One day, in a fit of enthusiasm, I lent the book to a
friend. It never came back.

Though the stories continued to haunt me, I did nothing about
getting another copy. The reason, I suspect, was that I missed the
book as much as I did the words and didn't want to read the stories
in any other edition. But from that day I became very stingy about
lending books. Can I blame my loss for that? Or is it, more probably, some defect of character which turns a bibliophile into a
bibliophiliac?

About a year ago, my wife found me another copy of the lost edition. It was exactly as I remembered it: the red cloth binding, jacket-
less, with its title in gold lettering on the spine, largish print, and a text
devoid of all critical apparatus. It felt, it smelt, just the same. When I
opened it, I half expected to find my name inside the cover.

Nostalgia is a dangerous indulgence. My rule is never to go back
to places or things I loved in childhood. It can lead only to disap-

---

H. G. Wells, *The Complete Short Stories* (Ernest Benn, 1927), is out of print,
but the following collections of his short stories are available: *The Country of
the Blind and Other Selected Stories*, ed. Patrick Parrinder · Penguin · Pb ·
464pp · £12.99 · ISBN 9780141441986; *The Complete Short Story Omnibus* ·
Gollancz · Hb · 976pp · £20 · ISBN 780575095243.

pointment. Even worse, reality erases the happy illusions that kind, unreliable memory has stored up for our lifelong entertainment. So the question was whether my recovered omnibus would bear re-reading. Would the Wells of memory be poisoned? After all, these 60-odd stories were already more than half a century old when I first read them, and now they were more than a century old.

I climbed on to my time machine, pushed the lever and rode fifty years back into the past to find, with surprise and delight, that Wells's world was just as I remembered it. He was as good as ever, but now I appreciated him even more.

The first thing to strike me was that Wells the writer, as opposed to Wells the prophet, has hardly dated at all. To be sure, the style is more deliberate than today's, the vernacular is different (and the word 'nigger' does occur at one point). And of course the London that Wells describes, with its thousands of smoking chimneys and horse-drawn barges on the Regent's Park canal, vanished long ago.

Why, then, does Wells sound so modern? Partly because he belonged to a generation in revolt against the high-flown rhetoric of late Victorian literature, but also I think because of his humble birth and socialist ideals. He came from a family of poor shopkeepers. He knew hardship, and the misery of a broken home, yet refused to employ his precocious talent in mimicking the affectations of the literary upper class.

The second thing to strike me was the extraordinary power of his imagination and his mastery of descriptive language. The finest example occurs in 'Under the Knife', the out-of-body experience of a man who submits to an operation which he is sure is going to kill him, and who finds himself hurtling towards the edge of the universe. The grim story of 'The Cone' tells of a taciturn steel-master who takes his wife's lover down to the works at dusk to admire the red and roaring drama of a blast-furnace at full throttle, and there exacts a horrible revenge.

Wells was a cunning writer. His miniature 'The Pearl of Love' –

it's only four pages long – is about an Indian prince who builds a temple to his dead princess. The sting in the tail of the story is unforgettable, the best I know. Wells is just as good at beginnings, hooking the reader in the first paragraph. Here, for instance, is the start of 'The Lost Inheritance':

> 'My uncle', said the man with the glass eye, 'was what you might call a hemi-semi-demi millionaire. He was worth about a hundred and twenty thousand. Quite. And he left me all his money.'
>
> I glanced at the shiny sleeve of his coat, and my eye travelled up to the frayed collar . . .

H. G. Wells makes the impossible believable by soothing the sceptical reader with crafty disclaimers. 'I have carefully avoided any attempt at style, effect or construction,' he writes in one place. And in another: 'I have been surprised at the credit accorded to the story . . .' Then you know he's about to confront you with an incredible proposition.

One of his tricks is to place the narrator among a group of friends listening to a tall tale while gathered round the fire after dinner. In 'The Time Machine', the story which made Wells famous, it is the Time Traveller who is 'expounding a recondite matter to us'.

> The fire burned brightly, and the soft radiance of the incandescent lights in the lilies of silver caught the bubbles that flashed and passed in our glasses . . . There was that luxurious after-dinner atmosphere when thought runs gracefully free of the trammels of precision.

Just as well. For the first words of the Time Traveller are: 'I shall have to controvert one or two ideas that are almost universally accepted . . .'

Sometimes the narrator is buttonholed by a man in the street. In 'The Diamond Maker' it is a ragged character on the Embankment who claims to have spent his last penny perfecting the manufacture of real diamonds in an unfurnished room in Kentish Town. The pauper takes out a stone the size of a thumbnail, offers it to the narrator for £100, and proceeds to tell his story, complaining that no one believes it. The narrator nearly does. And so do we.

By such devices the author puts clear water between himself and his readers, lulling them into a state of suspended disbelief. 'Is it just possible?' we ask ourselves. 'Perhaps, after all . . . ?'

So many of Wells's stories are about other worlds and other times that he is often described as a science-fiction writer – indeed, as a pioneer of the genre. But science fiction dates, and storytelling does not. And I think Wells's stories survive on literary merit alone.

True, his vision of tank warfare in 'The Land Ironclads', written in 1903, was prophetic. Wells's tank was not a tracked vehicle, however; it was based on the already-invented 'pedrail', a set of wheels with flexible feet attached to their rims, and it was a monster – a crawling fortress 100 feet long. His several stories about aeroplanes pre-empted the Wright brothers. But the picture of a twenty-second-century airliner which he drew in his novella of 1897, 'A Story of the Days to Come', was bizarre:

Mark Handley

an aerial galleon flying tiers of sails with passengers swinging in seats under its hull. In that story, the English countryside has been abandoned and there are skyscrapers, moving walkways and superhighways in the cities. But girls are still chaperoned and their fathers are still choosing husbands for them.

Wells used scientific themes not to predict the future, but to criticize the present. He is more Jonathan Swift than Arthur C. Clarke, more of a social seer (after the First World War increasingly a pessimistic one) than a futurologist. 'The Time Machine' is not really about time travel. It is a proto-socialist vision – much copied since –

of a world of extreme inequality in which an effete upper class drifts about enjoying the sunlight by day, but at night lives in terror of an underclass of cannibal brutes who toil in subterranean workshops. In his stark story of ritual sacrifice, 'The Lord of the Dynamos', the machine has replaced God.

Here is a scientific education being put to wonderful literary effect in stories which range far wider than science. There are ghost stories ('The Red Room') and monster stories, like the unforgettable 'Aepyornis Island', where a man is marooned with a giant hatching egg of the extinct Elephant Bird. There are stories of loss and regret ('The Door in the Wall') and stories of domestic life. There are morality tales: in 'The Country of the Blind', the one-eyed man is not king, but a handicapped immigrant. There are comedies, like 'The Man Who Could Work Miracles', in which the hapless Mr Fotheringay begins by willing a lamp to turn upside down in the pub and ends by nearly destroying the planet; and 'The Truth about Pyecraft', which turns on the fact that fat people never use the 'f' word but refer always to their 'weight'. There are even love stories: though I think these are the weakest. Wells may have loved women, but he wrote mawkishly about love.

They say it doesn't matter whether you read a story on paper or on a screen. But the loss and recovery of my Wells proved to me that books are 'more than a text' (to misquote Derrida). I cannot now imagine enjoying the short stories in any form other than the one I know, where book and text are bound – emotionally, literally and inextricably – together. I am glad to see that a new omnibus edition has recently been published, and I am grateful to scholars like Patrick Parrinder who have added so much to my appreciation of Wells, but I shall forever hold fast to my big red book.

CHRISTIAN TYLER's latest writing assignment involved a 2,000-mile train journey round Kazakhstan.

Shop with a Heart

MARIE FORSYTH

Every Friday afternoon I go to work in our local Amnesty second-hand bookshop, and each week I notice a shabby cover of a book entitled *If Jesus Came to My House* stuck on one of the walls. Few people see this unusual decoration as it is over the back stairs, with an admonitory notice next to it which reads, 'This slim tatty little volume sold for £30.' The book in question was sold by the shop's Internet team, and serves to remind the staff that they may not know what a book is worth until they start selling it to someone else.

With new and second-hand bookshops closing all over the country, how does our bookshop survive, flourish and send thousands of pounds to Amnesty International every year? Naturally it helps that all the books are donated and the shop is run by twenty-six volunteers. The Volunteer Co-ordinator told me during my induction that 'we have an entirely flat management structure. No one is more important than anyone else.' Anyone who has worked in an organization of more than two people knows that this has always been a Utopian dream, but it is still an admirable principle. It may also be necessary in this context as charity-shop work tends to attract retired people who can experience sudden health problems. 'We have three heart conditions here,' said the Co-ordinator imperturbably.

What is required of the voluntary staff? They clearly need to be literate and numerate and to have patience with the moodiness of the ancient till, but much of the success of the shop depends on those who have developed an appreciation of the monetary value of books which only comes with experience. A new volunteer with a working knowledge of Shakespeare, English poetry, nineteenth-century fiction and Booker prize winners will not know how to price a book called *A Dictionary of Poultry*. Or again, a title like *Medieval Church Screens of the Southern Marches* may not be universally appealing, but a check on the Internet shows that some people are currently prepared to pay £20 or more for it. Popularity has nothing to do with value, and the most prized books are often on rarefied subjects.

Not all donations are valuable but all are accepted. This does not mean that they will all be priced and shelved, but even the redundant encyclopaedias and out-of-date hotel guides are not wasted. The grimy and shabby, or those that have sat on the shelves too long, are parcelled up and collected by a recycling firm which pays a modest amount to take them away and turn them into fabric. Donors are encouraged to bring books to the shop in bags or boxes, but passers-by sometimes slip a couple of books round the door, announcing cheerfully, 'Got some more books for you!' Heavy loads may have to be collected by car. This encourages donations and is well worth doing, because the most interesting and valuable books are often found in personal libraries during house clearances. In the world of second-hand books the old and dusty are treasured not despised.

Our shop is small and space is at a premium. What kinds of books can profitably be sold? Serious book-lovers tend to look first at the section labelled 'Old, Interesting, Unusual, Collectable', a category which contains an eclectic mix of books, often with some rarity value. A large area is devoted to contemporary and popular fiction, where the paperbacks sell for twice the price of the hardbacks, because the hardbacks are twice as hard to sell. All items are priced at 50p in the children's section to encourage the young to read and grandparents to buy. The 3-year-olds choose *Peppa Pig* and their grandmothers buy *Black Beauty*. There are currently large sections devoted to biography, history, travel and health, and small sections to philosophy, humour and management studies. Local history books have no permanent section because they are always in demand. Copies of books already in stock may be allocated to the nearest hospice, while boxes of educational books find their way to a schools project in Sierra Leone. Less desirable books end up on the Bargain shelves at 50p. The main emphasis is on a swift throughput in all sections so there is always fresh interest for customers.

Occasionally I am tempted to think that the customers resemble the books, especially those that are well-worn, unfashionable and unexpectedly interesting. I once told an old man asking for Hungarian books that there was not much demand for them and that Magyar was a very difficult language. 'I know,' he said. 'It was my first language and I've forgotten it.' Some customers like to tell you who the book is for or why it's been chosen – a book about vinegar 'for my sister, because they say cider vinegar is good for arthritis'. Other customers have more romantic preoccupations. One starry-eyed girl asked if the shop stocked the white hardcover Nelson edition of *Pride and Prejudice* because she wanted her wedding ring to be placed on it during her marriage ceremony. Not everyone is charming or amusing. Long-time volunteers tell stories of past customers with 'anger management issues', or of the exhibitionist who dived into the sacks of unwanted books and then started to strip off to his underwear.

Anna Trench

The team launched an on-line shop in 2005 and now sells books all over the world, making a substantial contribution to the profits. Courtesy and speedy delivery are appreciated. One lady not only sent her thanks but also said what a pleasure it was that the parcel was 'addressed in educated handwriting'. Over 2,000 books are now kept in stock, perched perilously on the upper floors, and occasionally a human chain has to be organized to shift the books from one area to another. Each Internet book description says that all profits go to Amnesty International and many customers say how pleased they are to support the charity. The shop supports Amnesty financially without being part of its organization, but generous buyers may say 'keep the change' or make a small donation.

The bookshop is situated on a steep hill and parking outside is usually impossible. What persuades people to make the physical effort required to reach us? We see regular customers who are clearly addicted to books and buy by the bagful, and serious book buyers who are looking for bargains. We try to help those who have a definite quest and it is mutually satisfying when we find what they want. We recognize that some people just come in from the cold to browse and ruminate at leisure and that those who look a little lonely may need books as friends. Old books generate a special atmosphere which is both mentally stimulating and physically comforting: I can confidently say that none of us would get half as much pleasure and satisfaction from a room full of Kindles.

MARIE FORSYTH is surrounded by books at home and at work. Occasionally she feels the need to go into competition and write herself. She writes very slowly in French to friends in France and very quickly in English to everyone else.

Bibliography

Charity bookshops   91

Nicholas Crane, *Mercator: The Man Who Mapped the Planet*   32

J. P. Donleavy, *The Ginger Man*   39

The Folio Society   75

George MacDonald Fraser, *The General Danced at Dawn*; *McAuslan in
the Rough*; *The Sheikh and the Dustbin*   61

Ysenda Maxtone Graham, *The Real Mrs Miniver*   12

John Hegley, *Five Sugars Please*; *The Sound of Paint Drying*; *Uncut Confetti*;
Peace, Love & Potatoes   50

Clarice Lispector, *Near to the Wild Heart*; *Apples in the Dark*; *The Passion
According to G.H.*; *The Stream of Life*; *The Hour of the Star*   64

Malcolm Lowry, *Ultramarine*; *Lunar Caustic*; *Under the Volcano*   45

Benjamin Moser, *Why This World*   64

Irfan Orga, *Portrait of a Turkish Family*   7

Amos Oz, *A Tale of Love and Darkness*   23

Oliver Sacks, *The Island of the Colour-blind*   56

Josef Škvorecký, *The Cowards*; *The Bass Saxophone*; *The Swell Season*   18

Michael Swift and Angus Konstam, *Cities of the Renaissance World: Maps
from Civitates Orbis Terrarum*   32

The Times Comprehensive Atlas of the World (13th edition)   32

Horace Walpole: the letters of   69

H. G. Wells: the short stories of   86

Percy F. Westerman: the novels of   81

The *Slightly Foxed* Crossword No. 4: Answers

Across: 1 PAGE; 3 NGAIO MARSH; 9 QUILP; 11 BEING A CUB; 12 ONE ARM;
13 ETHIOPIA; 15 FACEY ROMFORD; 18 SOAPEY SPONGE; 21 TINCKHAM;
22 MILLER: 24 EX-BRITISH; 25 SMITH; 26 EX-SATANIST; 27 STAR

Down: 1 PEQUOD; 2 GRIMES; 4 GIBB; 5 IDIOT-PROOF; 6 MAGGIE MUGGINS;
7 ROCK POOL; 8 HUBBARDS; 10 PAR LAGERKVIST; 14 PERSUASION; 16 AS IT
WERE; 17 BARNABAS; 19 ELLIOT; 20 ARCHER; 23 THUS

Coming attractions . . .

PAUL ATTERBURY meets Inspector Appleby

YSENDA MAXTONE GRAHAM gets caught in the rye

PATRICK MERCER joins the night-runners

PENELOPE LIVELY returns to Alamein

ROHAN CANDAPPA falls into slumberland

JUSTIN MAROZZI travels with Norman Lewis

ANDREW MERRILLS finds himself betwixt woods and water

TESSA WEST sets out her stall

The Royal Society *of* **Literature**

15 April Richard Mabey on Nightingales

13 May Roy Foster, Edna O'Brien and Grey Gowrie discuss Yeats's poetry (in collaboration with the British Academy, to be held at the Irish Embassy, London)

17 June Neil Gaiman on his life and work

The RSL hosts regular talks, discussions and readings. Fellows and Members are invited to attend any of these meetings. Members of the public are also welcome to attend. There are up to 30 tickets for non-members at each event, which are sold on the door on a first-come-first-served basis from 6 p.m. for £8 (£5 concessions). All meetings begin punctually at 7 p.m., and are held in the Kenneth Clark Lecture Theatre, Courtauld Institute of Art, Somerset House, Strand, WC2, unless otherwise stated. For booking information visit www.rslit.org, call 0207 845 4677 or e-mail hazel@rslit.org. Membership of the RSL is open to all. Please call us on 020 7845 4676 or visit our website for further information.